DOUBLE POST BASKETBALL:

Offensive Power and Fundamentals

DOUBLE POST BASKETBALL:

Offensive Power and Fundamentals

John Stiver

Parker Publishing Company
West Nyack, New York

© 1982, *by*

PARKER PUBLISHING COMPANY, INC.

West Nyack, N.Y.

Library of Congress Cataloging in Publication Data

Stiver, John,
　　Double post basketball.

　　Includes index.
　　1. Basketball—Offense. 2. Basketball coaching.
I. Title.
GV889.S74   1982　　　　　　796.32'32　　　　　82-12507
ISBN   0-13-218891-0

Printed in the United States of America

DEDICATION

I would like to dedicate this book to my wife, Becky, and to my daughter, Jennifer.

Also to the fine young men I have had the privilege to coach.

To Rick Strunk whose time and patience were invaluable in editing the book.

To my fellow coaches who have shared their knowledge with me.

HOW THIS BOOK CAN HELP YOU

This book presents a basketball offense that is fundamentally sound against either the man-to-man defense or a variety of zone defenses. It furnishes ideas and methods that make the offense successful. All patterns and special plays illustrated in this book have been proven in actual competition. This book is an effective reference guide for a new coach who is looking for an offensive plan; it offers the experienced coach a change in strategy.

Four major areas that make up the foundation of this offensive plan are: (1) high percentage shots, (2) organized movement of the ball, (3) organized movement of the players and, (4) floor balance. The basic philosophy of the offense requires that all five players be involved in the offense with the purpose of obtaining a high-percentage shot.

The Double Post Offense consists of three series: the strongside series, the weakside series, and the post and clear series—all signaled by the point guard. Each series can be run as a patterned offense in itself. When the patterns are run with patience, a strong inside game results and high percentage shots develop. This deliberate phase of the offense allows your team to keep the pressure on superior teams.

The Double Post Offense can also be run as an "organized" free-lance to strike at the defense with quick one-on-one and two-on-two plays. These free-lance options give the players opportunities to use their individual offensive talents to create openings in the defense. Combining the patterns and free-lance options make the offense very difficult to scout.

The Double Post Offense can be used at all levels of competition. The degree of execution, however, at the different levels of play may vary. Parts of this offense are played and accepted everywhere, but the organization of the parts is original.

The most unique feature of the Double Post Offense is its simplicity. The offense is divided into two groups—perimeter and post. This helps specialize coaching assignments and make understanding the system easier. The entire offense is based on basic individual moves, two-man situations, and three-man situations. Chapters 2, 3 and 4 are devoted to the development of these offensive fundamentals.

The Double Post Offense can be used against any zone or combination defense as shown in Chapters 9 and 10. Using the same basic pattern repeatedly has led to better execution against all defenses and saves time that can be used on learning fundamentals.

Chapter 11 deals with the fast break. The fundamentals of defensive rebounding, outlet passing, player distribution, end break situations, and transition into the double post offense are covered extensively.

Special situations are covered in Chapter 12. The idea is to be prepared for every possible situation. Quick scoring out-of-bounds and jump ball plays are presented. Successful methods of attacking full- and half-court presses are described and fully illustrated in Chapter 13.

Every phase of the Double Post Offense is based on sound fundamental techniques. It is the proper execution of the fundamentals that makes the offense effective. That is why I have included the drills and practice organization that I use to facilitate the teaching of our offensive system. All the fundamental skills of passing, dribbling, shooting, ball handling, rebounding and conditioning that are practiced during our sessions to develop the complete player are included.

You definitely will find something to add to your game style, because the Double Post Offense offers a sound fundamental approach to winning basketball.

John Stiver

CONTENTS

1

Installing the
DOUBLE POST
System

One of the most important decisions a coach must make each year is what offensive system to use. Some coaches use a different offense each year, while others put players in a formation and let them free-lance.

The Double Post Offense permits the players to free-lance, yet it allows you, the coach, to have control over the offense. (I consider the offense an "organized free-lance.") There are only three basic patterns to learn, built on two- and three-man situations. The following pages illustrate how to build the Double Post Offense step by step, thoroughly and completely.

REASONS FOR SELECTING THE DOUBLE POST OFFENSE

The Double Post Offense was developed with the following points taken into consideration:

1. Flexibility in using offensive personnel

It permits you to use two big players in the pivot position. Many teams have more than two tall players that they would like to use at the same time but neither one can play forward. The Double Post solves this problem by placing two big players close to the basket.

This system allows you to play with one small player, two larger forwards and two centers. This offense is suited to an outstanding point guard.

Three guards and two centers provide more speed in the lineup for pressing and fast-break situations, or for better ball handling in control situations.

This sytem also permits you to play with two guards, one forward and two centers.

2. Specialization of coaching assignments

In a junior high or high school situation, the staff is usually composed of one varsity coach and one JV coach. This makes it necessary for the varsity coach to organize practice sessions to teach the required skills. Since most gyms are shared with other teams, utilization of practice time is very important.

By dividing the squad into either the perimeter or post, you can assign one group shooting drills and work the other group on fundamental drills pertinent to their positions. All fundamental drills are broken into these two categories.

3. Better offensive rebounding

Rebounding assignments are easier to teach from a double post set because the two big players are closer to the basket. Offside rebounding is handled by a post player instead of a forward. Also, the opponent's forward must cover a post, which is to your advantage. Our statistics on rebounding have proved that our Double Post Offense gives us the advantage.

4. Point Guard has at least four entry passes

Depending on which double post formation is being used, a point guard can have two, three or four possible entry passes each time he dribbles down the floor to initiate the offense. This puts pressure on the defense because they cannot readily recognize from where the offense will start.

Also, most coaches can teach one or two players a variety of moves to bring the ball up-court against pressure. We practice daily against pressure to insure that we can start the offense.

5. Offense can start by a pass, dribble, screen or drive

Being able to start the offense is one of the most important areas of the offense itself. The point guard can start with a pass, dribble, screen or drive; any of the four is all right. The point guard has built-in choices depending on what type of defense is applied; the other four players react according to his response. In any case, the offense is provided with a number of entries that prevent the point from making an incorrect choice.

6. Fundamentals

The Double Post Offense is fundamentally sound. The offense is broken down into the basics of shooting, passing, dribbling, and moving without the basketball. After individual skills are learned, two- and three-man situations successful to all offenses are taught. These situations are then incorporated into the Double Post Offense. Our offense is based on executing the fundamentals correctly.

BASIC ALIGNMENT OF THE DOUBLE POST OFFENSE

1-2-2 Formation

In Diagram 1-1, the initial alignment is a 1-2-2 set. The point, 01, starts the offense in the key area. The two wings, 02 and 03, line up at the free throw line extended, approximately 15 to 18 feet from the basket. The posts, 04 and 05, line up on the blocks on each side of the free throw line. It makes no difference in which position the wings and posts set up because the offense is mirrored.

One of the essential tasks of developing a successful offense is assigning players to positions that best suit their talents. A coach must

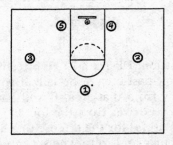

Diagram 1-1

know the strengths and limitations of his players if he wants his offensive systems to be successful. It is necessary to teach skills to the players and then fit the offense to their abilities.

The initial alignment is given to the players on the first day of practice, so that they know the ideal spot for each position. Each player is taught how to obtain the correct position so that the entry pass can be made.

The Double Post Offense makes use of seven different formations. Some double post sets are more advantageous against some teams than others. Also, your talent is going to change from year to year and different sets can take advantage of the skills on hand. Since the same offensive rules apply to all formations, it also makes it easier for the players to understand what is expected of them. If you run three basic patterns from one formation, you have merely presented the defense with three situations, but if you run three plays from seven different formations, you have given the defense 21 different situations.

1-3-1 Formation

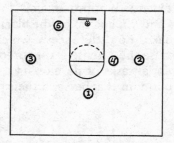

Diagram 1-2

The 1-3-1 formation (Diagram 1-2) is effective against teams that cannot defend the low-post area, especially if you have a player who can score consistently from that area. If you have a player who is a good jump shooter and driver from the foul lane area, this is a good set to use. This set is useful for the offense that likes to run give-and-gos, backdoors, and pick-and-rolls. The set cannot be defended by a team that likes to run-and-jump and double-team.

1-4 Formation—High or Low

The 1-4 high formation (Diagram 1-3) is a good set to run if wings, 02 and 03, can drive by their men for easy shots, or if the posts, 04 and 05, can cut to the basket and attack inside pressure. This offense set is commonly used against all zones.

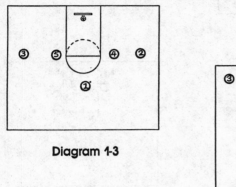

Diagram 1-3

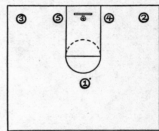

Diagram 1-4

The 1-4 low formation (Diagram 1-4) is used when you have an excellent point guard (01 position) that can dominate his defender by either driving or shooting the short jumper. If you are having trouble with man-to-man pressure, use this alignment. It is a good set for flash cutters.

Double Stack from 1-2-2

This is a good set from which to begin the offense, especially against good pressure defense (Diagram 1-5). This set allows for crackdown screens to release the wings. It is a strong formation for attacking close to the basket.

Double Stack from 1-3-1

This formation (Diagram 1-6) takes advantage of weaknesses in the defense's covering of your posts, 04 and 05. When you need two points and want a score from your inside players, you go with this formation.

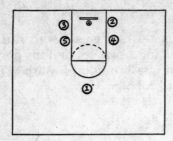

Diagram 1-5

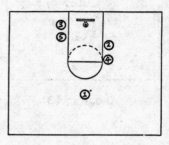

Diagram 1-6

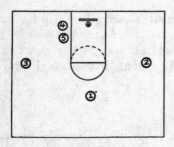

Diagram 1-7

Unbalanced Stack

We use this formation (Diagram 1-7) when there is a mismatch at one of the wings, 02 or 03, and if one of our posts can beat his man continually.

The formations are called verbally: "number 12" for 1-2-2, "number 13" for 1-3-1, "number 14 high" or "number 14 low," "number

12 stack" or "number 13 stack," and "unbalanced stack." Quickly changing formations distracts the defense and works to your benefit.

THE POINT MAN

The point man, 01, should be able to bring the ball up-court against pressure and start the offense approximately six feet from the top of key. He should be in a position where the offense can be started to either wing or post man. The point man should be smart, alert, quick, and possess a good understanding of what is to be accomplished on offense. He must be skilled in picking up weak areas of the defense and attacking them.

Since the point guard starts most offenses with a pass, he should be an excellent passer. He should also be a good driver with the ability to shoot over a screen. The point guard must be skilled in a variety of one-on-one moves to allow him to advance the ball against pressure and to score from the top of the key. We use constant pressure in our daily practice to build confidence.

We train three point guards. Usually the number two point guard is one of the startng wings and is a junior. This enables us to have an experienced player at the point postion and at the same time build for the future.

THE WING MEN

The wing men, 02 and 03, must also be able to bring the ball up-court against pressure. Each wing should be able to play point on occasion. We want the wing to receive the ball foul line extended.

The wings should be excellent shooters, so a great deal of time must be spent on spot shooting drills daily. Each player is given an assigned shooting program. (Most coaches simply assume players can shoot, but do not structure their shooting drills around the type of shots you obtain from your offensive system.)

Along with assigned shooting, a variety of one-on-one moves must be practiced daily from the wing position. Wings are also expected to post all mismatches, therefore time must be spent with low-post moves.

Wings are expected to rebound and are drilled daily on this. This is one area where most coaches could increase the amount of time spent on offensive rebounding.

THE POST MEN

The post men, 04 and 05, position themselves on the block on each side of the foul lane. It is the post's responsibility to post up to receive the ball in the low-post area.

Both post men should be strong rebounders. Jumping, rebounding and tipping must be drilled daily. Size is not always a factor— toughness and willingness to mix in crowds are, however.

The post men are taught a variety of moves with their backs to the basket and moves from the high-post area. We expect the posts to be good passers as well as adept at setting proper screens to and away from the ball. Establishing a good inside attack is essential to playing winning basketball. Forcing the defense to cover the inside yields medium-range jump shots for your perimeter players.

The post men will be used to change alignment to give your players the most advantageous offensive position. The post men must be taught several counter moves based on how the defense plays them.

WAYS OF BEGINNING DOUBLE POST OFFENSE

Most coaches have only one or two ways to start their offense, and when the defense takes these cuts away—they have nothing. Rigid patterns take away many scoring opportunities. We teach several methods and let the player pick the best route, based on how the defense is playing him.

We will show each of these cuts from a 1-2-2 set, but you should see how these cuts can be used with any of the other double post formations. During practice sessions, we use different formations to start the offense. The players then learn the movements from all formations.

Our first offensive rule states: After passing the ball, move to a new floor position. Since our offense begins with a point guard, he has several choices for starting the offense. The point guard always has the first cut; this minimizes confusion and helps coordinate the offense.

Diagram 1-8 shows a sideline, (A), straight, (B), and a strongside cut, (C), which are used when the point guard, 01, wants to form the strongside triangle. The sideline cut, (A), is used when the defensive man is pressuring and forcing him outside. When the defender is

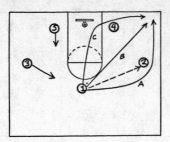

Diagram 1-8

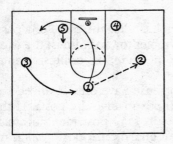

Diagram 1-9

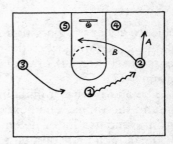

Diagram 1-10

applying pressure to force the point inside away from the pass, then the strongside cut, (C), is made. This is just a simple give-and-go. The straight, (B), is the quickest way for the point to get to the corner and is not used very often.

The weakside cut (Diagram 1-9) is used to counter our strongside cuts. It creates space for the wing to penetrate and work various two-man plays with the post. This is an especially strong way to start the offense if the defense is not doing a good job of defending the post area. All of these maneuvers will be discussed in detail in Chapter 7.

If we feel that either of the wings can beat his man one-on-one, the point will pass and screen opposite. A switch usually occurs between the defensive men. This is a good maneuver to use if you want to create a mismatch in size or speed at the wing position. Also, the point, 01, can roll back toward the ball for a possible jump shot.

In Diagram 1-10, the point, 01, is dribbling to the wing position. If the point man cannot get the ball to a wing or post by passing, he

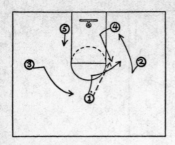

Diagram 1-11

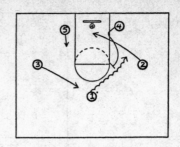

Diagram 1-12

dribbles to either wing position. The dribble takes the place of a pass. Our rule for the wing when the point dribbles toward him is: the wing slides to the corner, (A), or clears to the other side, (B), as illustrated in Diagram 1-10.

The above ways of initiating the offense have only involved the point and the wings. The next two methods involve the posts. If the wings are under a lot of defensive pressure, the post men automatically break to the side post or if the point guard calls "post" (Diagram 1-11). The point, 01, passes to the post, in this case 04; the onside wing, 02, breaks backdoor, and the point rubs off of 04. These movements start the post series. The other method, clear, is initiated when the posts break up and the point cannot pass to them or when the point calls "clear." As shown in Diagram 1-12, the post, 04, sets a screen one foot above foul lane on side post; the onside wing, 02, clears and the point, 01, dribbles off the screen—a simple pick-and-roll.

In order to keep the floor balanced—regardless of which of the above methods is used to initiate the offense, the players will always end up in either an overload or a 1-2-2 alignment. This is very important for your players to understand, because the offensive situations are based on these two formations after the first pass, dribble or screen. This also aids in organized offensive rebounding and organized defensive floor balance.

GENERAL RULES OF OFFENSE

Keep the floor balanced at all times. Each of the above formations after the first pass, dribble or screen provides us with the following conditions: After each shot one-and-a-half players are playing defense and three-and-a-half players are on the offensive boards. There is always continuous designed movement. Offensive rebounding positions are organized on the positions of the players.

Always keep 12 to 15 feet between players. This allows each player freedom to move, but permits the ball to be reversed without difficulty. As a player cuts, another fills his spot. This adds continuity.

Each player is to pass first, drive second and shoot third. We want our players looking for the best available shot each time down court.

Only high percentage shots are taken—players must know what their percentage shot is and work toward obtaining this shot. If a bad shot is made, it is more difficult to recover from a missed shot.

To insure coordinated movement between all players, the following offensive rules are enforced strictly:

1. The point, after passing the ball to a wing or post, moves to a new floor position. The point will always make the first cut.

2. The wing or post, after receiving the ball from the point, plays with the point.

3. The post will always make the second cut. He must watch and see what the point does, read his defensive man, and make one of his combination moves. These moves will be discussed in Chapter 4. The post men must be aware of the pressure on the wing.

4. Weakside wing will always assume the point position after the point makes his cut. This is important for two reasons: a.) defensive responsibilities, and b.) maintaining position for continuing the offense if the ball is reversed.

2 Developing the Complete
DOUBLE POST
Offensive Player

The Double Post Offense stresses the individual skills of all players, regardless of position. All players in the program are taught the same fundamental skills that are presented in this chapter. Regardless of what style of offense you use, you can improve your team's effectiveness by developing the complete offensive player. No team offense is stronger than its weakest offensive player.

BALL HANDLING

The first area to work on each day at the beginning of practice is ball handling. Players must develop a feel for the ball. The ball must become so much a part of the player that he is aware of it even though he cannot see it.

Form a circle in the middle of the court and give each player a basketball. At the beginning of the season the emphasis of the drill is on correctness rather than quickness. As the players progress with the drills, stress quickness. Practice will develop good ball-handling skills. Following are the ball handling drills to perform daily:

1. *Pound the ball*. Hold ball in one hand and pound into the other hand (10-20 repetitions).

2. *Finger tip drill*. Hold the ball on the finger tips with the arms extended shoulder high. Tip the ball back and forth between the hands while moving the arms up and down (10-20 repetitions).

3. *Pass ball around ankles, waist and head*. Bring feet close together and pass the ball around the left side with the left hand to the right hand and around to the front again. Start with the ball around the waist, then move the ball around the ankles, up toward the head, and pass it around. Continue to move ball up and down around the body (5-10 repetitions).

4. *Single leg circle*. Spread feet about two-and-a-half feet apart. Start the ball in the left hand in front of body, pass the ball and bring it around the right leg to the front position in the left hand. After 10-15 repetitions around the right leg, start around the left leg.

5. *Combination—around legs and body*. Combine drills 3 and 4 above.

6. *Figure-eight between legs*. Start the ball in the left hand and put it between legs to where right hand can receive the ball. The right hand then passes the ball around right leg and back through between legs to left hand. The left hand then passes the ball around left leg. This movement continues for 10-15 repetitions.

7. *Figure-eight with drop*. Start this drill as in the figure-eight. Bring ball around left leg with left hand and continue to swing it on around in front to right hand, which carries ball around right leg and through legs from the back. Both hands are holding the ball momentarily, then drop the ball to the court and quickly exchange hand positions by bringing right arm around in front and left hand in back. Hold the ball with two hands and continue (10-15 repetitions).

8. *Side catch*. Hold ball between legs with right hand in front and left hand in back. Then drop the ball, quickly exchange hand positions and catch the ball before it touches the court. Continue this movement back and forth (10-15 repetitions).

9. *Front catch*. In a crouched position, hold ball with both hands behind your legs, drop ball and quickly move both hands to the front of the legs to catch it . Then reverse the movement to catch ball in the original position (10-15 repetitions).

10. *Spin the ball on one finger*. Spin the ball on one finger and keep the ball spinning by hitting the ball on the side with opposite hand.

11. *Dribble around one leg*. Assume a position with right knee on the court and left leg bent. Start with ball in right hand, dribble the ball under left leg to left hand; the left hand dribbles the ball around the front of left leg to right hand. This continues for 10-15 repetitions, then change to dribble around right leg.

12. *Dribble figure-eight around legs.* Assume a position with legs spread. Starting with ball in right hand, dribble ball between legs to where left hand receives the ball and dribbles it around left leg. The left hand then dribbles ball between legs to where right hand receives ball and dribbles it around right leg. The drill continues for 10-15 repetitions.

13. *Front pockets.* Hold ball with both hands waist high, drop ball, slap hands on legs where pockets are, and catch ball before it touches the court (10-15 repetitions).

14. *Side pockets.* Same as above, except slap hands on hips and catch ball (10-15 repetitions).

15. *Back pockets.* Same as numbers 13 and 14, but slap hands on back pockets before catching ball (10-15 repetitions).

16. *Crab run.* Assume a crouched running position and start with an exaggerated long stride. While stepping out with the left leg, place the ball under the thigh. Continue down the court as fast as possible without dropping the ball. On the way back, run backwards in a crouched position in an opposite manner from the first forward run, in which the ball was passed under the legs. Go down and back the length of the court twice. This drill is especially good for tall players.

DRIBBLING

Dribbling is an important offensive maneuver. It is used to advance the ball from back court into the offensive area when passing is not feasible. The dribble is used to move away from defensive pressure. Last of all, the dribble is used to beat the defense one-on-one in the scoring area.

All players like to dribble, but this is the basketball skill that is most often abused. You must not only teach the fundamentals of dribbling, but also the proper attitude. Too much dribbling destroys the team concept that is so important in a successful basketball program.

First practice the ball-handling drills, then form four lines of three players at one end of the court as shown in Diagram 2-1. Each different dribble is performed twice going up and down the court. For simplicity, each drill is described using the right hand.

General guidelines for teaching dribbling

1. The player must keep his head up and his eyes looking straight ahead to be able to spot the open man.

2. Control the ball with the finger tips.

3. Each player begins his turn at performing the drill with his weak hand. The goal is for each player to dribble proficiently with both hands.

4. Free arm (non-dribbling arm) is slightly up and flexed. It serves as a protector.

5. Move as fast as possible while still maintaining control over the ball and body.

Speed dribble. The purpose of the speed dribble is to advance the ball quickly downcourt when there is no defensive man nearby. The body must be upright and the ball must remain in the right hand. The player pushes the ball ahead and down to the side of his body while running after it full speed. After the player dribbles the length of the court, he places his left hand on the court and continues to dribble with his right hand in a circle, pivoting on the left hand. After one rotation he comes up and dribbles the ball with the left hand as he returns to his line.

Change-of-pace dribble. The purpose of the change-of-pace dribble is to get the defensive man to slow up or straighten up when the dribble slows up. When the defensive man reacts, the dribbler speeds by his man. In teaching the change-of-pace dribble, the player speed dribbles for about 20 feet. After speed dribbling, he changes to a control dribble. After two or three control dribbles he accelerates with the speed dribble. He continues to use the same hand until he reaches the end of the court and returns using his left hand.

Crossover. The purpose of the crossover or change-of-direction dribble is to bring the ball in front of the player while he looks straight ahead. This allows him to see the open man. He dribbles to the right with the right hand for three dribbles and pushes off with his outside foot (right foot) and makes a slight pivot on the ball of his foot at a 90° angle. The right hand should push the ball across in front of the player. The ball is now in the left hand. The player continues downcourt, crossing over every three dribbles at 45° angles and making 90° cuts.

Between-the-legs dribble. The purpose of this dribble is to change direction against tight defensive pressure with less chance of error. The player dribbles three dribbles at a 45° angle. At the end of the three dribbles, he bounces the ball between the legs from his right hand to his left hand under his left leg. He pushes off with his right foot and pivots with his left foot. He should not lose any strides while performing this dribble. The player continues down the court dribbling between legs every three dribbles at 45° angles and making 90° cuts.

Behind-the-back dribble. This dribble allows the player to change direction while facing his opponent. The ball is protected by his body. The player again dribbles at a 45° angle. After his third dribble he executes the behind-the-back dribble. The ball should be pulled back behind the body with the right hand and bounced to the left hand. Again, as in the between-the-leg dribble, he pushes off with the right foot and pivots with the left foot. The player continues as in the previously mentioned dribbles.

Reverse. The purpose of the reverse is to change direction against defensive pressure to ball side and to keep the body between the defensive man and the ball. In practice, at the end of the third dribble, the player dribbles to the right, pushes off on the inside foot (left foot), pivots on this foot and swings around the right leg to cut defensive man off. The player pulls the ball with his right hand until the pivot is made, then picks up the dribble with the left hand and moves forward. If the dribbler switches hands too quickly, the ball is left out where the defender can easily steal it. To prevent the flick, the dribbler must maintain control of the ball with one hand until he completes the pivot and dribbles in a new direction. Always beware of a possible double team or run-and-jump defensive maneuvers.

Fake reverse. The purpose of the fake reverse is to have an alternate dribble against an overly aggressive defender who does a good job against a reverse. Do everything the same as in the reverse, but on this dribble, when the player's position and ball are halfway into the reverse move, he comes back to his beginning position and moves forward with control.

In all these dribbling drills, the players do not encounter any defensive pressure. The last phase of developing dribbling skills will be against defensive pressure from different areas of the court. These one-on-one dribbling situations will be discussed in Chapter 3.

STOPS AND PIVOTS

Before a player can pivot, he must know how to stop quickly with good balance. There are two methods of stopping with the ball: the two-foot jump stop and the stride stop. The feet hit the floor simultaneously in the two-foot jump stop. The feet should be shoulder-width apart with the knees bent, and the body weight low to withstand the stop. The two-foot jump stop has the advantage of using either foot for a pivot foot.

In the stride stop, the player is running in a slight crouch. He lowers his hips as his rear foot hits the floor, which becomes the pivot foot, while the other foot follows.

Pivoting is a very important fundamental movement. Basketball players pivot after they receive a pass, come to a stop after dribbling, and rebound. They also pivot after the two-man play such as the screen-and-roll, or after the three-man play pass and screen opposite.

1. *Front Pivot.* The front pivot is executed when a player jump stops and uses his left foot as the pivot foot, and steps forward and around facing the desired direction. The ball is held chest high in a position to protect, pass, shoot or drive.

2. *Reverse Pivot.* The reverse pivot is executed with a jump stop. The player uses his left foot as a pivot foot and swings the right foot back facing the desired direction. The ball is held as in the front pivot.

Line Pivot Drill. The players form four lines of three at one end of the court. The first player in each line dribbles to an area foul line extended, jump stops, executes either a front pivot or reverse pivot, passes to the next player in line, and then moves to the back of the line.

Circle Pivot Drill. Line up players as shown in Diagram 2-1. The first player in each line dribbles towards the coach, stops, pivots, and passes to the first player in the line in the direction of the pivot. After the pass, the player moves to the end of line to which he passed. The drill continues until all players have pivoted in both directions.

Stopping and pivoting drills should be practiced each day, and

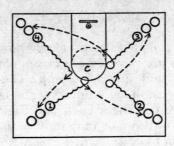

Diagram 2-1

should not be run more than two minutes at a time. The drills should be fast paced.

SCREENING

Screens are important in the Double Post Offense. The proper technique of screening is often overlooked when teaching players how to move through offensive patterns. All players must understand how to set a screen, and how to cut or dribble off the screen.

Screening provides two important functions: (1) It frees a player for a scoring opportunity, (2) it forces a defensive switch that creates a mismatch.

The screening techniques that are taught to the players are the screen-and-roll, screen-away, and dribbling screen. When teaching screening techniques, emphasis also must be placed on cutting off the screen so that the timing of the play situations are successful.

Screen-and-Roll. The offensive player has the ball. He sets his defensive man up either by looking at the basket or faking a drive. The player setting the screen moves directly to the defensive man and sets himself perpendicular to the defender. This position will force the defender's shoulder to make contact with the center of the screener's chest. The screen should be set as close as possible without making contact. The defender is allowed a normal step. The screener holds the screen until there is contact with the man he is screening. The player with the ball does not move until the screener has become stationary. The driver should dribble close enough to the screener to make contact with him. The first dribble or two is usually the best time to pass to the roller. The screener, upon making contact with the defender's chest, reverse pivots, making contact between his buttocks

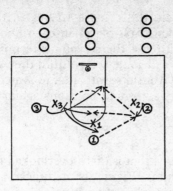

Diagram 2-2

and the defensive man's legs. The reverse pivot should be made towards the basket with the lead hand extended and ready to receive a pass. The roll should be made so he can see the ball at all times. The driver has the options of driving for a lay-up, shooting a jump shot, or passing to the roller.

Screen-Away. The screen-away is used away from the ball to free a player breaking toward the ball for an easy shot. Freeing a player with this type of screen requires accurate timing between the cutter and screener. For the screen to be successful, the cutter must occupy his defensive man by making a movement in a direction opposite the intended cut. The screener must concentrate on the defensive man and not dead space. The screen should be set as close as possible to the defender with his body perpendicular to the defensive man. The cutter should make contact with the screener as he breaks off the screen toward the ball. If a switch occurs, the screener should front-pivot into the cutter's defensive man and move toward the ball, looking for a pass.

Dribble Screen. The offensive player with the ball dribbles toward a player and that player sets his defensive man up for a screen. The dribbler drives the ball to the inside of the cutter, comes to a two-foot jump stop, and makes a flip pass to the cutter. The player can drive for a lay-up, shoot a jump shot, or make another dribble screen. If a switch occurs, the screener rolls to the basket.

Drills. To teach the proper techniques of screening, line the players as shown in Diagram 2-2. After the offense scores or loses possession of the ball, the offense rotates to the end of the line, defense to offense, and first player in each line plays defense. The offensive players must use the screening techniques of screen-and-roll, pass-and-away, or dribble screen until they score. The defensive pressure is changed from no switching, to switching, and to sagging which teaches proper screening positions against varying defenses.

PASSING

Passing is an area that is often overlooked or given only a small amount of practice time. Passing is the quickest means of advancing the ball up-court. Regardless of what type of offensive system you may wish to develop, a well-planned system of practice on passing will cut down the number of turnovers and create high percentage shot opportunities. Every coach should *demand* excellent passing. Poor passing is usually a result of poor coaching discipline.

General guidelines in teaching passing

1. Always thank a player for a good pass that leads to a score.
2. Players should never telegraph their passes.
3. Never pick up a dribble unless the player for whom the pass is intended is open.
4. The ball should have a little backspin on it, making it easier to handle.
5. Pass away from the receiver's defensive man.
6. Avoid the long crosscourt pass.

The following types of passes are emphasized in our Double Post Offensive system: two-hand chest pass, two-hand bounce pass, two-hand overhead pass, baseball pass and flip pass.

Two-hand chest pass. The chest pass is probably the most commonly used pass. It is used for short distance passing and for getting the ball into the offensive area and to the post men. Hold the ball close to the chest with elbows into the sides of the body. Make the pass with a forward thrust of both arms and a snap of the wrists outward.

Always follow through with the arms. It is especially helpful to the beginning passer to shift the weight forward with a forward step. Aim the ball at the chest of the receiver. How hard the pass is thrown depends on the distance the receiver is from the passer.

Two-hand bounce pass. The bounce pass is a slower pass, but is a good pass to use at the completion of a fast break and is effective in getting the ball to the high or low post. Hold the ball and make the pass in the same manner as the chest pass. The difference is that the ball will strike the floor a few feet away from the pass receiver so that it will bounce up to the waist for easy handling. A disadvantage to this pass is that it can be easily intercepted.

Two-hand overhead pass. The overhead pass is an excellent pass to use to feed the post men in the pivot or in passing over the head of a defensive player. Hold the ball with the hands on the sides and with the arms extended over the head. Point thumbs inward. Make the pass with a snap of the wrists and a forward motion of the forearms.

Baseball pass. The baseball pass is used to make a long pass downcourt or to get the pass out to start the break. The technique for this pass is the same as the baseball throw. The right-handed passer brings the ball behind his right ear. The right hand is behind the ball with fingers spread and the weight is shifted to the right foot. As the pass is made with a forward motion of the arm and wrist, the weight shifts to the left foot. Follow through with the arm fully extended and with a straight-down snap of the wrist, so as not to curve the pass.

Flip pass. The flip pass is used in close quarters. The pivot player uses this pass to feed cutters and the dribbling screener uses it to pass to players cutting by the screen. Hold the ball on the side of the body away from the defensive player. Give the ball a slight upward flip with the wrist which causes the ball to move softly into the air. It is easily handled by the receiver.

Receiving the ball. When teaching the fundamentals of passing always emphasize receiving the ball, because a pass must be properly received before it is successful.

Emphasize the use of both hands. The ball should be caught with the

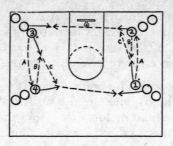

Diagram 2-3

finger tips, with a slight give of the arms so as to soften the pass. For all passes below the waist, the finger tips should be pointing downward when catching the ball; in all passes above the waist, the finger tips should be pointing upward.

Drills for Passing

Two-Line Passing Drill. This drill is used to teach the proper fundamentals of passing and receiving. The players are in two lines with each player facing a partner, 10 to 12 feet apart. Each pair of players has a ball and works on the two-hand chest pass, two-hand bounce pass and the overhead pass.

Single Line Drill. To get the players to move after the pass, use the single line. The players are in two lines and pass the ball from one line to the other. Each player then moves to the back of the other line. The two-hand chest pass, two-hand bounce pass, overhead pass and flip pass are practiced and each pass is made within the center circle.

Three-Man Passing Drill. This drill forces the players to fake one way and make the pass by a defensive man. The squad is divided into four groups of three players with a defensive player between two offensive players who are 10 feet apart. The player who has the ball attempts to pass by the defensive man. After successfully making the pass, he becomes the defensive man and the defensive man assumes his position. The drill continues in this fashion.

Four Corner Passing. The four corner passing drill teaches the players to pass and follow, but sharpens quickness and reaction skills. The squad is divided into four groups (see Diagram 2-3) and a group

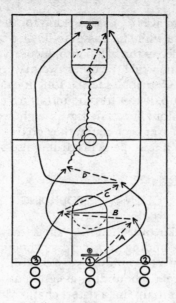

Diagram 2-4

is placed at each corner of the half court, approximately 15 feet apart. Start the drill with two basketballs diagonally across from each other. Player 01 starts the drill by making a chest pass to 02. Player 02, after receiving the ball, passes back to 01 who has advanced for a short pass. As soon as 01 receives the return pass, he makes a two-handed touch pass back to 02. Player 02 passes to the player behind, 03, and goes through the same procedure. While 01 is going through the routine, 03 is going through the above procedure at the same time. As the drill is learned, a third and fourth ball are added, which makes for a very snappy drill.

Ball in the Ring. Here is a drill in which the ball is moved quickly around the circle with a defensive player. The squad is divided into two groups of six. Each group forms a circle of five players with a defensive man in the middle of the circle. The ball is passed by or around the defensive player. If the defensive player intercepts the ball, he takes the passer's place. The passer cannot pass to the player on his immediate right or left.

Figure Eight. The players form three lines under the basket (Diagram 2-4). Player 01 starts the drill by passing to his right and cutting behind the receiver who is breaking for the pass. The receiver, 02, continues to move while he passes to 03 and then cuts behind 03. Whichever player receives the ball past half court, in this case 02, must dribble to the foul lane while the other two players, 01 and 03, fill the outside lanes. Player 02 dribbles to the foul line and bounce passes to 03, who shoots a lay-up. Player 01 rebounds the ball and passes back to 02 who stayed at the foul line. The figure-eight weave continues back down court. As the players get better, they go two, three or four times up and back without a mistake. This drill is also good for developing the fast break.

OFFENSIVE REBOUNDING

Few teams make over half the shots they attempt, however, strong offensive rebounding can increase shooting efficiency. Many coaches plan defensive rebounding very carefully but leave offensive rebounding to chance. (Rebounding assignments for the Double Post Offense will be taken up in a later chapter.) Before you assign offensive rebounding responsibilities, however, you must teach individual technique.

The offensive player has several means available to him to neutralize the defensive player who is attempting to box him out. First, knowing when a teammate is likely to shoot and where the ball is likely to bound gives the offensive player an opportunity to avoid getting blocked out. An offensive rebounder can crowd the defender's inside position, causing him to lose his balance.

An important key to offensive rebounding is to never stand still when the shot is taken—this makes it hard for the defense to block out. The determination to continually go after the ball is also essential. We teach two techniques that are central to good offensive rebounding: the back spin and roll, and fake-and-go opposite.

Back spin and roll. Use this technique when the offensive player is completely blocked out. The offensive rebounder reverse pivots on one of his feet, rolls off the opponent's back, and positions himself parallel to the opponent.

Fake and go opposite. The offensive rebounder anticipates being blocked out and fakes first toward the opposite direction in which he intends to go. The defensive rebounder commits himself and the offensive rebounder is free to find the missed shot.

The following drills are used to teach the fundamentals of offensive rebounding:

Second effort drill. Each player touches the rim or some spot on the backboard as many times as he can for 30 seconds. Record his score each time he works out.

Tipping. Each player taps the ball off the backboard using his left hand 10 times, right hand 10 times. Alternate hands 10 times.

Offensive tip drill. Divide the squad into two groups of six at opposite ends of the court. You can work one group while the manager works the other. Position yourself on the opposite side of the lane with three basketballs. Throw the basketball off the board so that the first player in line tips the ball into the basket while it is still in the air. He rebounds his own tip-in, places the ball next to you and returns to the end of the line. The drill continues.

One-on-one rebounding. Place two players in the lane area; one will play offense and the other, defense. You start the drill with a shot at the basket. The defensive player must box the offensive player out. The offensive player attempts, by any means available (back and spin, or fake and go opposite), to get the ball and score. The drill continues as the defensive player becomes the offensive player and the offensive player goes to the end of the line. (This drill may be used to teach defense, also.)

SHOOTING

Good shooters are made, not born, and they are made through hard work. This statement emphasizes to players the necessity of learning the correct fundamentals of shooting and of spending time in organized practice to develop these habits.

For the last six years, as a team we have shot between 46% and 49% every year. I feel that our practice format has led to this good shooting percentage.

All my players must be clear on two areas: (1) each player must know what his high-percentage shot is and from what distance he can shoot it, and (2) each player should practice the type of shots suited for an offensive system.

Without going into an in-depth shooting discussion (this is a topic for a separate book), we want to offer some pointers that we emphasize during our practice sessions.

Shooting Pointers:

1. Balance the body before attempting a shot.
2. Always square the body to the basket.
3. Hold the ball in the finger tips on the palm of the hand. Spread the fingers with the index finger in the center of the ball.
4. Use the off hand to balance the ball with the shooting hand. The off hand does not interfere with the shot, but serves as a guide.
5. Keep the elbow in close to the side.
6. Flex the knees with weight on balls of feet.
7. The ball is in the correct position if the player can see the bottom of the ball and sight the rim at the same time.
8. As the shoulders move the arms up, the forearm moves toward the basket. Release ball from the finger tips as the wrist is snapped downward with the index finger pointing to the basket.
9. Follow-through is very important; it indicates that the ball has been shot correctly.

As you develop your shooting practice, take the following thoughts into consideration. Organize practice—good shooting is developed during practice. Pick out spots on the court from which your players are going to get good shots, then practice from these areas. Practice standing still, off the pass, and off the dribble. Shoot against pressure, simulating game conditions.

Drills for Shooting

Beginning drill. Pair the players and give each pair a basketball. Have the players shoot the ball to each other emphasizing the proper techniques.

Two-line lay-up drill. To practice lay-ups, use the two-line drill. Half of the squad lines up on the sidelines at center court with the other half on the sideline. The first player in the line dribbles to the foul line, jump stops, and bounce passes to the first man in the right line, who cuts to the basket for a lay-up. The passer rebounds the ball and passes to the shooter, and the shooter passes the ball to the next player in line. This drill resembles the ending of a two-on-one break and also is used in teaching the fast break.

Standing jump shot drill. Form one line 12 feet from the basket. Each player shoots, rebounds his own shot and passes to the next person in line. The coach corrects shooting fundamentals.

We use a number of shooting drills throughout the season, but most of them are used in the development of perimeter and post men, or fast-break situations, all of which will be dealt with in later chapters.

FAKES AND DRIVES

One of the most difficult areas to teach is one-on-one offense. If a player is going to contribute to your offense, he must develop some kind of proficiency at beating his man. In teaching fakes and drives three moves are fundamental, all using the same pivot foot. They are jab and shoot, jab and go, and jab and crossover.

Before learning these three moves, a player must learn to assume a triple-threat position after receiving the basketball. Emphasize the following areas when teaching triple-threat position:

1. Get open to receive the ball while in shooting range. This makes you a threat.
2. After receiving the ball, *face the basket*. Be an offensive threat.
3. Place the ball between the waist and chest. This forms a triple-threat position, which allows you to shoot from the outside, fake and drive, or pass the ball.

Do not let the players put the ball on the floor upon receiving it. Too many scoring opportunities are wasted by doing this.

Jab and shoot. Make a short jab fake toward the basket as though driving. Position the ball outside the right knee with both hands (right hand on top of ball). Back the defensive man up to protect the basket. If the defensive man backs up sufficiently by the fake, return to your original position and shoot a jump shot. Make sure your head is up and balanced at all times.

Jab and go. This move begins like the jab and shoot. Make a good jab step toward the basket. If the defensive man does not react to the jab step, extend your right foot, push off with your left leg and explode to the basket.

Jab and crossover. This move begins with the same fake. Make a good jab step toward the basket. If the defensive man reacts to cut off your drive and also stays close enough so you cannot shoot the jumper, then you cross over. Do this by pivoting on your left foot, then swing the ball over to your left with a low, quick movement and at the same time cross over with your right foot. Place your right foot as close to the defender's right foot as possible. As you put the ball on the floor, you can pick up your pivot foot and drive to the basket. Be careful that your pivot foot leaves the floor after you dribble the ball or you will be called for walking.

To teach the mechanics of the jab moves, use a one-line drill which starts at the foul line. Place a chair at the foul line in the lane area. Each player attacks the chair with jab and go, jab and crossover, and jab and shoot moves. While the players are performing these moves, you can correct them.

After the players have an understanding of the jab moves, let the players go one-on-one from the foul line. Form two lines, one under the basket and one at the foul line. The players under the basket play defense and the players at the foul line work on their one-on-one moves. The drill starts when a player under the basket rolls the ball to a player at the foul line, then charges the offensive player. The offensive player reacts to the defense with his one-on-one moves. The players are only allowed six dribbles. This keeps the drill moving quickly. As long as the offensive player scores he continues to work the defensive player. This makes the defensive player really work. When the offense no longer scores, the players exchange lines and the drill continues.

OFFENSIVE MOVEMENT WITHOUT BALL

Meaningless movement within the Double Post Offense must be eliminated. In order to free our players to receive a pass from another player, we teach several offensive cuts without the ball to keep the offensive area from getting congested.

Principles of Movement

1. The first movement should be slow, setting up the defender for a quick change of pace at full speed.
2. All cuts are made at right angles and straight lines.
3. The offensive player should be under control so that he can stop quickly.
4. All cutters must give a target when moving toward the ball.

The following situations illustrate the different moves that can be made from any position. The situations are based on how the defense plays his man.

1. *Backdoor Cut.* When the defensive man is overplaying toward the ball, the receiver should take three steps toward the ball. On the third or fourth step, he plants the left foot, pivots and pushes off hard to cut behind the defender to the basket. He extends the right hand for a target.

2. *V Cut.* If the defensive man is playing to back side, the receiver will break toward the goal with three or four steps, plant the right foot, pivot and break hard to meet the pass, extending the left hand for a target.

3. *Hook Cut.* If the offensive player is close to the sideline, he will break toward the side of the foul line. The player should plant his right foot, pivot and move to meet the pass, and extend the left hand for a target.

4. *Reverse.* If the defensive player is playing tough, it might take a combination of moves to get open. The offensive player should take two steps toward the ball, make a backdoor cut for three steps, and V cut back out to receive the ball.

5. *Middle Cut.* Any time an offensive player can cut between his defender and the ball, a middle cut is used. This cut usually results in a high percentage shot. It is not always necessary to make a fake before the cut, although, if the defender needs to be set up for the cut, the player does so. He moves away from the ball, then breaks over the top of the defender to receive the ball.

To teach these moves a defensive man is assigned to guard the receiver and is told to deny the ball. The receiver must move to get open and to get the ball in a designated area which is chalked on the court. Each player will go one at a time for three rotations. After the offensive player receives the ball, he goes one-on-one, working on his jab moves. This drill is run from different areas on the court so players will become familiar with receiving the ball from different areas. This is a very important drill that all players need to learn to master the necessary skills to get open to receive the ball.

QUICKNESS DRILLS

Every coach wants to have quick players, but each of us knows this is not possible, especially at the junior high and high school levels. Quickness is a natural attribute so it becomes a hard-to-teach area. However, each coach can improve a player's reaction time by putting him through a series of stations that demand repetition of skills as quickly as possible. These drills not only improve reaction time, but also improve conditioning, endurance, jumping, and second effort. These drills only take six to eight minutes of practice and are well worth the time.

Our quickness drills consist of 12 stations, with as many repetitions as can be performed in 30 seconds. The manager uses the score clock and sounds the buzzer every 30 seconds, signaling the players to go to the next station. Each player records the number of repetitions on a sheet located at each station upon completion of that station. After the quickness drills are completed by each player, the manager picks up all sheets and makes up a composite of each player's effort. The total number of repetitions for all stations are added together and divided by 12. This gives us a Quickness Index of the average repetitions performed each 30 seconds. You will be surprised at the rate of improvement as the season progresses, and at who the quickness players on the team are.

The following are the stations we use for our quickness drills (Diagram 2-5).

1. *Toss-Back lay-up.* A Toss-Back is set up four feet from the middle of the side of the lane. The drill starts with a player at the foul line. He passes the ball to the Toss-Back, moves quickly to receive the

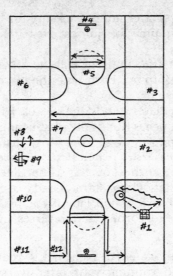

Diagram 2-5

return pass, shoots a lay-up, gets his own rebound and speed dribbles back to the foul line.

2. *Rope jumping.* Player skips on two feet as fast as possible. Each jump is a repetition.

3. *Tipping.* Player stands just in front of the backboard to the right of the basket. He tips the ball ten right, ten left and ten alternating as many times as he can for 30 seconds. Each tip is a repetition.

4. *Hook shot.* Mikan drill for 30 seconds. Each made shot is counted as a repetition.

5. *Lateral line drill.* Start at the side of the foul line and laterally move back and forth across the lane. Each time across lane is one repetition.

6. *Short jump shot.* Player stands with one foot to the right of the basket. On the buzzer, he shoots jump shots on the right side, then on the left side. He continues in this manner and each made shot counts as a repetition.

7. *Crosscourt sprints.* Player stands at the midcourt dividing line, sprints forward across court to other out-of-bounds line and runs backward to the original position. Each time across court is one repetition.

8. *Line jumping*. Player jumps back and forth over a marking line on the court. Each time he jumps over the line counts as one repetition.

9. *Harvard step drill*. Pull out bleachers part way if you do not have a bench to step up on. Each time the player steps up counts as one repetition.

10. *Rim touches*. Player stands one step back from front of rim. He takes one step and touches rim. If the player cannot touch rim, use the backboard. Each time rim or backboard is touched is one repetition.

11. *Bench jumping*. Use a bench 15 to 16 inches high. Player jumps back and forth over bench as quickly as possible.

12. *Defensive sprints*. Player starts at end line and moves laterally to foul lane, back pedals to foul line, laterally across lane, sprints forward to endline, laterally to corner, and reverses procedure to starting position.

Developing fundamental skills helps reduce the number of turnovers committed running your offensive system. By spending time each day developing quickness skills your players will improve as the season progresses and with each year the players are in the system.

3

Perimeter Position
Coaching for the
DOUBLE POST
Offense

The continual development and improvement of the perimeter players for the Double Post Offense should be a primary concern in your planning. The perimeter players must be able to control the game offensively through their skills. Since there are so many situations in which a post man will handle the ball away from the basket, against pressure or on a fast break, the post men must also develop some of the same skills as the perimeter players. Post players must spend extra time before and after practice developing these skills.

The program for perimeter development consists of dribbling against pressure, point-to-wing passing and wing-to-post passing, perimeter cutting, offensive moves from the wing position and drills to develop shots from the Double Post Offense.

QUALITIES TO DEVELOP IN THE PERIMETER POSITION

The qualities that the perimeter players need for the Double Post Offense to be successful are

1. Quickness of performance in offensive maneuvers.
2. Controlled passing and dribbling skills against intense pressure to initiate the offense.
3. Ability to control the tempo.

4. Ability to recognize the defense and make the correct offensive adjustments.

5. Ability to shoot the medium jump shot standing, dribbling and off the screen.

6. Ability to get open to receive the ball at the wing position.

7. Confidence to score from one-on-one moves from the wing position.

DRIBBLING AGAINST PRESSURE

Getting the basketball into the offensive area to initiate the offense is the most important function of the perimeter players, especially the point players. Use the following procedures to teach players to encounter pressure.

There are four dribbles that the perimeter players must master. They are the sprint or speed dribble, crossover dribble, reverse dribble and change-of-pace dribble. These have been explained in the preceding chapter.

Three-Quarter Court Dribbling Drill

Begin the drill at the top of key at the far end of the court. The players pretend there is defensive pressure. They dribble through the center jump circle and execute a speed dribble, with a lay-up off both feet. This type of lay-up is used because it provides more control and better rebound position if the shot is missed. After executing the speed dribble—twice with the right hand and once with the left hand—practice the crossover, reverse and change-of-pace.

Blind Dribble

This drill is performed in pairs, and starts at half court. Player 01 dribbles the ball with his eyes closed while 02 breaks anywhere he wants toward the basket. When 02 shouts, 01 must pass to 02. Player 02 can shoot a lay-up or jump shot. The drill continues for one minute.

The last stage in the development of dribbling skills is our one-on-one drills from full court, three-quarter court and half court. Each player must make dribbling moves to advance the ball up-court against strong defensive pressure. This drill should be as close to a game situation as possible.

For one-on-one full court, the offensive player has the ball in the backcourt at the baseline. He uses either a jab-and-go or a jab-and-crossover move to advance the ball up-court. He takes a lay-up or jump shot if he beats the defense.

Three-quarter court one-on-one is called a bust-out drill. The defensive player lines up in the middle of the center circle, while the offensive player starts at the top of key in backcourt. The offensive player dribbles hard at the center circle, trying not to be forced to the sidelines by the defensive player. He proceeds to go one-on-one for a jump shot or lay-up.

Our half-court one-on-one drill is run from three different areas: right wing, left wing, and foul line. One line of players lines up under the basket—this is the defensive line. The other players line up at the top of the key, forming the offensive line. The first defensive player in line rolls a ball to the first offensive player. The defensive player charges the player with the ball. The offensive player must react to the charge and make the appropriate move. For instance, if the defensive player charges left, the player drives right; if the defense hangs back, the player shoots the jump shot. The offensive player cannot dribble more than five times. As long as the offense scores, he keeps the ball; the defense must try to stop him.

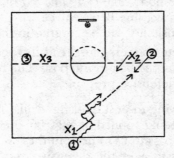

Diagram 3-1

PERIMETER PASSING SITUATIONS

Once the players have developed the basic skills of passing, simulate game situations that are related to the success of the offense. Many of the offensive situations in this book depend upon the entry pass from the point to the wing.

The "Point Entry" drill is designed to teach the point to get the ball to the top of the key and keep the dribble alive before the pass is made to the wing. It is also used to teach the wings to get open and receive the ball no farther out on the court than the foul line extended, as illustrated in Diagram 3-1.

The drill is performed as follows: 01, the point man, has the basketball at the center jump circle with a defensive man; 02 and 03, wing men, line up on foul line extended with two defensive men overplaying them. The point man starts the drill by attempting to dribble the ball to the top of the key against strong defensive pressure. At the same time, the wing men attempt to get open by a V cut, hook cut or reverse cut. When a wing frees himself, the point should execute a crisp pass. Upon receiving the ball, the wing squares up at the basket. If the defensive man overplays in a position that denies entry to the wing, the wing executes a backdoor cut.

The next passing situation involves the wing-to-post pass. Players must be taught how to get the ball into the post. It is important that the ball go into the low-post area, since it usually results in a high percentage shot.

The following points are emphasized about feeding the post from the perimeter:

1. The wing is responsible for establishing the correct passing angle to the post, called the *line of deployment*, which means there is a direct line between the wing and the basket. The post's responsibility will be covered in the next chapter.

2. The perimeter players must read the position that defense is using to deny the ball to the post. The ball should be passed away from defensive pressure.

In the first wing-to-post passing drill, 02 has the ball with defensive pressure being applied by X2 from the wing position. Player 02 is attempting to pass to 04, who is in the low-post position. Player 02 has to use fakes to alter the defensive man's position before he passes to 04; he cannot dribble. Rotation in the drill is: 02 goes to defense, defense goes to 04's position, 04 goes to end of line and next player takes 02's position.

The second drill has 04 positioned at medium post with a defensive player applying pressure from the foul line side. Player 01 passes to 02, 04 is the offensive player, and 02 then passes to 04. Player 04 executes a power lay-up. Rotation in the drill is: 01 takes 02's position, 02 takes the defender's place, 04 goes to the end of line and the next player takes 01's position.

The third drill has 04 at medium post with the defensive player applying pressure from baseline side. Player 01 passes to 02, 04 pins the defense, 02 passes to 04, who executes a power lay-up. Rotation is the same as in the previous drill.

The success of the wing-to-post pass involves the player establishing alignment with the post, reading the defense, and knowing when to pass. Only by practicing these situations can the players understand what you expect of them.

PERIMETER CUTTING AND SCREENING

In the Double Post Offense it is essential that the perimeter players know how to get open for a shot or a pass, and how to set their defensive men up to rub off a screen. Teach the following movements to the perimeter players so they can utilize one-on-one moves, offside screens, split-the-post and flash cuts.

Utilize the V cut concept. Teach the players to read the defense, move toward the pressure and break opposite. If the defensive man is playing high on the offensive man, the offensive man takes him several steps higher and then cuts low. If the defensive man is playing low, the offensive man takes him several steps lower and then cuts high. In both situations, as the offensive player receives the ball he attempts to score.

Perimeter players should always be ready to make backdoor cuts to the basket if overplayed. The two backdoor situations to be prepared for are (1) overplayed on wing, and (2) overplayed on point. In the first situation, player 02 steps towards ball, plants his left foot, and cuts hard to the basket, extending his right hand for a possible pass. In the second situation, the weakside wing has moved to the point to reverse the ball and is overplayed by his defender, X3. Player 03 steps towards the ball, plants his right foot, and cuts hard to the basket, extending his left hand for a possible pass.

The offense uses both vertical and horizontal screens. For the screens to be effective it is necessary that the cutter set his defensive man up before he rubs him off.

Diagram 3-2 shows a vertical screen being set by 01 on X2, who is playing high. 02 takes his man several steps higher and cuts off the screen, making sure to rub shoulders with 01. Diagram 3-3 shows another vertical screen being set by 01 on X2, who is playing low. 02 sets his man up by taking him lower and then cuts off the screen

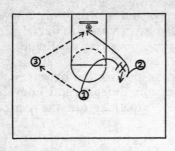

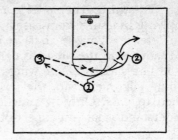

Diagram 3-2   **Diagram 3-3**

making sure to rub shoulders with 01. 02 should be open at the foul line for a jump shot.

Diagram 3-4 shows another vertical screen used when the perimeter players split the post. Player 02 passes to 05, steps towards the point, and screens X1. 01 steps towards the baseline, setting up X1 for 02's screen, then cuts off the screen rubbing shoulders with 02. 05 can pass to 01 for a jump shot or to 02, pivoting toward the ball after the screen for a jump shot.

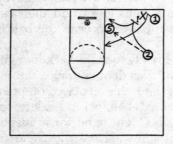

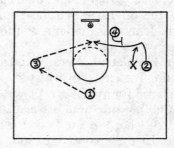

Diagram 3-4   **Diagram 3-5**

The horizontal screen is used when a perimeter player rubs his man off a post player (Diagram 3-5). It is 02's responsibility to set his man off. If executed properly, a lay-up or short jump shot results.

To counter tough defensive pressure in the wing area, the perimeter players are taught several release moves. The wings, 02 and 03, can cross along the baseline. This move can also be made from the 1-2-2 or 1-3-1 double stack alignments. The baseline screen is shown in Diagram 3-6. This is a strong move to get the ball to a perimeter player with good one-on-one moves. By also clearing the onside post,

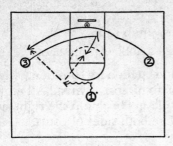

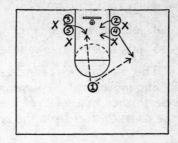

Diagram 3-6   **Diagram 3-7**

the perimeter player has plenty of room in which to operate. Diagram 3-7 shows the wing, 03, breaking into the lane when his defender plays on the outside of the stack. If the post defender switches to prevent the quick pass to 02, the post, 04, breaks to the wing area for the pass from 01.

Our screening situations are drilled through three-on-three situations. After the players understand how the screens are executed, they are free to choose the correct cut to get open. To make the drill competitive, we play possession.

MOLDING THE OFFENSIVE WING PLAYER

To make the Double Post Offense successful, it is important to have wing players that pose an offensive threat. Not every wing player is going to be an outstanding shooter or driver, but it is up to you to teach the player to have confidence to become an offensive threat.

In developing wing players, spend time on driving the baseline and driving the middle from both sides. The purpose of the following drills is to develop offensive ability and confidence.

Perform all of the drills in a series of five from both sides of the court. To simplify teaching, right-handed players use their left feet as pivots and left-handed players use their right feet. A chair or towel is used as a defender. All lay-ups on the right side are shot with the right hand and those on the left side are shot left-handed.

Jab Moves

    1. Jab, drive, lay-up

    2. Jab, crossover, lay-up

3. Jab, jump shot

4. Jab, drive two or three dribbles, jump shot

5. Jab, crossover, over two or three dribbles, jump shot

The jab moves originate from a stationary position, while dribbling moves make a player more of an offensive threat. All moves are performed in a series of five. The players begin on the right side of the court 25 feet from the basket. Use both sides of court.

Dribbling Moves

1. Dribble right hand, cross over to the left, lay-up

2. Dribble left hand, cross over to the right, lay-up

3. Dribble right hand, change-of-pace, lay-up

4. Dribble left hand, change-of-pace, lay-up

5. Dribble right hand, reverse, lay-up

6. Dribble left hand, reverse, lay-up

7. Dribble right hand, between legs, lay-up

8. Dribble left hand, between legs, lay-up

SHOOTING DRILLS TO DEVELOP HIGHER PERCENTAGE PERIMETER SHOOTERS

Plan shooting drills so that players practice from the areas that they are going to shoot from. Have them shoot from standing position, moving position and game-simulated situations with the use of the toss back.

Spot Shooting or Standstill Shooting

Stand in a perimeter area 12 feet to 15 feet from basket and take five shots at a time from different spots on the perimeter. For example, at each side of baseline, two shots; at wing position foul line extended, two shots; and top of key, one shot. Change five spots each time you do the drill. Do not move to another spot until you have made five shots. Players work in pairs, one rebounding and one shooting.

Twenty-Five Jump Shots Drill

This is a shooting drill to do every day. It is a great drill for developing consistency in shooting if done properly. Player 01 is the shooter. He must concentrate on the mechanics of his shot. He must try to receive the pass, square himself to the basket, jump straight up, execute the shot and follow through, land on balance and move again. This drill requires constant motion; player 01 must never stand still. The breakdown of the 25 shots is as follows: 5 no dribble—jump shot, 5 one dribble—jump shot, 5 head fake then dribble—jump shot, and 10 combination of all dribble moves—jump shot. Remember, 02 is the passer. His job is two-fold. First, he must study 01's shot to make sure he is shooting correctly and second, he must keep 01 moving by passing the ball quickly and, at times, away from 01. Players should make at least 13-25 shots.

Toss-Back

Use the toss-back to simulate four possible shooting situations that usually develop from the perimeter offense. The situations are: splitting the post from wing to post and baseline to post, plus the pinch post from both sides. Each player shoots three from each situation.

Beat a Pro

This is really a fun drill, yet it is challenging. Object of the game is for your player to score 12 points before the pro he is competing against scores 12. The game begins with a foul shot. If your player makes it he gets 1 point; if he misses, the pro scores 3 points. Your player then takes jump shots from various spots on the floor and for each basket he makes, he gets 1 point. Each time he misses, the pro scores 2. Whoever gets to 12 first wins. (Note: If your player made the first shot he must shoot a minimum of 68% to beat the pro. If he missed the first shot he must shoot a minimum of 70%.)

4 Developing the
POST POSITION

The key positions in the Double Post Offense are the post positions. The offense is structured to attack from the inside-out. A constant inside concentration puts pressure on the defense. The inside attack stresses options that are executed inside the lane area.

The basic philosophy for developing the post position is:

1. Post men are closer to the basket, providing higher percentage shots;

2. Post men have more opportunities for three-point plays;

3. Post men can control the backboards.

This philosophy has remained constant regardless of the size of the post players.

Following this post program not only develops your tall players but makes your shorter post players "play tall." We have had players ranging from six feet to six feet eleven inches play in this position. The program for post development consists of teaching the proper area for low and high post, improving position for receiving ball, catching the ball, combining post movements without the ball, and developing moves from the low post and high post.

GENERAL RULES FOR POST MEN

1. Maintain contact to make a quick, accurate decision offensively—you must know where the defender is and how he is playing you. To do this you must maintain contact. You

establish contact with your inside arm, butt, and back.

2. Always keep arms above head when moving in the post area so that you are ready to receive a pass or grab a rebound.

3. When you are side fronted knock the defender's arm away with your inside arm.

4. Demand the ball.

5. Play with authority and aggressiveness.

6. Dominate your man.

Low-Post Area

The low-post area is located above the rectangle along the side of the lane. We refer to this area as "The Block." Setting up between the "block" and the next lane marker will give the low post the best angle from which to attack the defense. A variety of shots can be attempted from this area, but the three to concentrate on are the short jump bank shot, drop step with a power shot, and a short hook shot from the middle of the lane.

High-Post Area

The high-post area is located in any one of three spots along the free throw line—both high side posts, and the middle. The offense utilizes the high side post the majority of the time. This position provides a good angle from which to set screens, feed the low post, run two-man plays, and use jab moves to score. Occasionally, you can flash a wing into the high-post area.

POSITIONING

Positioning is the most important aspect of low-post play. Each square inch of the low-post area is vital territory. The battle for position requires a great deal of physical and mental toughness. The most important aspect of positioning is setting up quickly, and this requires quick movement on every possession.

The post men's position in the low post should be as follows: knees bent—maintain a bent knee position; slight bend at the waist;

hip against the defender; arms up at shoulder height; elbows bent at right angle; and hands up and open. The arm closest to the defender should be a little lower and in contact with the defender. The post man must hold his position with his hip—making sure that arm and side do not push the defender. The arm on the open side should extend out a little and give a good target.

Improving Post Positioning

The most important fundamental in improving post position is to force the defensive man to move toward the side he is playing. Moving the defender will create more room for the pass to the open side.

To force the defender to move, try to keep the foot closest to the defender even or slightly ahead of the defender's lead foot. Use legs and body weight to move the defender and do not push with the arms.

In order for the post man to establish position to receive the ball in the low-post area, he must understand how to position himself against a defense that is playing behind, front, baseline side, and foul line side.

1. If the defense plays in *front* of the post, the post should force him away from the basket to create more room for the lob pass.

2. If the defense plays *behind*, the post should set up along the edge of the lane so that he can receive the ball as close to the basket as possible. This position gives the post a variety of moves against the defense.

3. If the defense plays on the *foul lane side*, which usually occurs when the ball is at the wing position, the post should set as high as possible to create more room for the pass baseline side.

4. If the defense is located on *baseline side*, the post should force him as close to the baseline as possible to create more room for the pass to the foul line side.

The same techniques for positioning against the low post are utilized at the high post. The only difference is that the players should not force their defender too far down the lane or too far toward the point area. This can crowd the low-post area.

The post men must understand how the defense will play them in the high post area. This is usually determined by whether the ball is located at the point position or at the wing position.

1. Ball is located at the point position.
   a. If the defense fronts the high post, it usually leads to an easy basket. The post man must seal the defender off and break quickly to the basket.
   b. After the defender gets beaten several times, he will play either behind or to the side of the post. As a general rule, after receiving the ball the high post is to turn and face the basket. This position gives the post several options. He may (1) pass to the low post; (2) look for the jump shot; (3) drive; or (4) pass to the opposite side of the floor.
2. When the ball is located at the wing position, the defender will play the high post in a side fronting position. The same options as mentioned above in 1b are used.

CATCHING THE BALL

The catch is not always made in the same manner; it depends upon the defender's position. Two of the most common receiving situations are catching the lob pass and catching the direct pass.

Whenever the ball is lobbed over the defender, the post should hold his position until the ball has cleared or is even with the defender's head. He should then release and go to the ball. A premature release will give the defender an opportunity to close the gap and to shrink the target area for the passer. Do not push off.

Always try to catch the direct pass with two hands. If the pass is away from the defense and you are holding the defender off properly, you will have to learn to catch the ball with one hand. This is a one-hand block catch in which the ball is immediately clamped with the free hand. Bring the ball close to your body immediately and hold it at eye level.

COMBINATION MOVEMENTS WITHOUT THE BALL

Post men operate in a restricted area, so they must move with a purpose in order to get open to receive the ball. Movement without

purpose is wasted motion, so here are several maneuvers to coordinate the movements of post men.

The post men are responsible for changing alignments and
varying their cuts to keep the defense honest. The post moves are
really a separate offense in themselves. Chapter 2 discussed various
one-on-one moves to attack the defense with purpose. You should
now apply this knowledge so that two post men can perform in a
coordinated manner.

When the point brings the ball across midcourt, the post men
should be in constant movement—movement that will keep the floor
balanced, put your post men in a position to receive the ball, and make
it difficult for the defense to play the posts honestly. Some of the
movements employed by the posts are

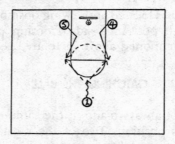

Diagram 4-1

1. *Break from the low post.* In Diagram 4-1, point man 01 crosses
   midcourt, 04 and 05 make a short jab step toward the center
   of the lane with their inside feet, push off with those feet and
   break toward the side high-post area. The post should receive
   the ball with a jump stop.

2. *Low-post interchange.* Posts 04 and 05 interchange positions
   and one or both can break toward the high side.

3. *X move.* Posts 04 and 05 break diagonally to the high-post
   areas on the opposite sides.

4. *High-low screen.* This maneuver is employed whenever we want
   to get the ball to the low-post area with a possible mismatch.
   Post 04 would be the taller player. In the down screen, the low
   post, 05, steps towards the baseline, plants his left foot and
   quickly cuts over 04's screen to side high post to receive ball.
   04 reverse pivots on his right foot, putting the defender on his

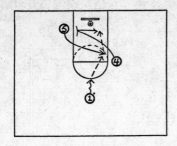

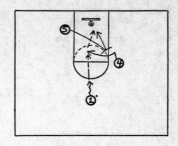

Diagram 4-2   **Diagram 4-3**

back looking for a pass from 05 (Diagram 4-2). Diagram 4-3 illustrates the up screen. Post 04 steps toward the baseline, plants his right foot and quickly cuts over 05's screen to the low post to receive ball. 05 reverse pivots on his left foot and moves toward the basket for a possible pass from 04.

5. *Stack.* The stack alignment is used to create a mismatch or switch between the defensive post men 04 and 05. Diagrams 4-4 and 4-5 illustrate two possible situations of the stack.

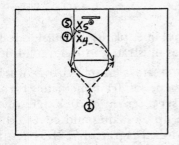

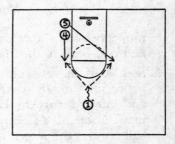

Diagram 4-4   **Diagram 4-5**

Whenever the ball is passed to the wing, the onside post has four options:

1. *Post 04 can position himself at low post on ballside.* If onside post is in the high-post area, he can slide down to the low-post area.

2. *Fan.* Post 04 is being defended foul line side, and cannot receive the ball. He slides down the side of the lane for two steps and moves across to the weak side. Post 05 is positioned halfway up the lane on the weak side. At the same time, 05

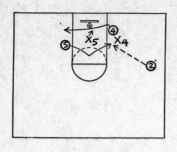

Diagram 4-6

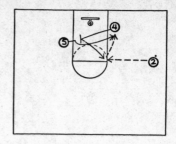

Diagram 4-7

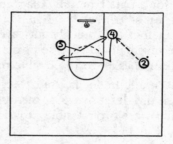

Diagram 4-8

moves two steps towards the foul line, plants his outside foot and cuts hard to the low post as illustrated in Diagram 4-6.

3. *Roll.* This move is utilized to create a mismatch or switch between 04 and 05's defensive men. Post 04 immediately turns and moves across the lane to set a screen on 05's defensive man. 05 sets his defensive man up by faking and cuts to the ball around the screen as shown in Diagram 4-7. If 04 sets a good screen and there is a switch, he has the option of rolling back to the ball for a possible pass from wing 02. Post 04 can shoot the jump shot or pass to 05 at low post.

4. *Away.* Post 04 moves up the side of the lane and across the lane to the weak side. Post 05 moves his defensive man several steps in the direction he is playing and breaks to the ball as shown in Diagram 4-8.

It should be very apparent that these maneuvers help establish a total inside game. These combo movements make it very difficult for the defensive men to play your post men honestly.

Use the "Post" movement drill to teach the combo moves of fan, roll, and away. First practice the maneuvers with the defensive men and you call a particular move. Then, add two defensive post men who go through each of the three basic cuts. The defense will vary its coverage. The post men are allowed to score and use any offensive moves to get open.

MOVES AND SHOTS FROM LOW POST

The move and type of shot will depend upon your player's position and the defender's position, but the post should be going to the basket whenever possible. The post should also be going for the three-point play to put pressure on the defense. This is an active part of the offensive game plan.

When receiving the ball, the post should know where the defender is. This will come as a result of the contact he has with the defender and the direction of the pass.

1. *Power move.* If the defender is playing on the foul line side, the post should force him higher, give the target on the baseline side, and use a quick drop step and power the ball to the square above the rim. No dribble is necessary. He should keep the defender on his back, shoot the ball from slightly in front of his head and make the defender reach over him to block the shot.

2. *Baseline slide with power dribble.* Again the defender is playing foul line side. This time the post is a little further up the lane; the defender is a little more behind and the post receives the ball with both feet on the floor. To avoid a travel, he must dribble and drop step toward the rim. In the drop step, wrap the baseline leg around the defender so that this contact will keep him pinned on your post man's back. The power dribble should be hard and right between the legs. Keep it close to the body.

3. If the defender is playing baseline side, the post forces him lower to increase the target area for the pass. Since the post will need to make his move to the middle of the lane, he must be more aware of helping defense. The basic moves to the middle of the lane are

   a. *Drop step with power lay-up* as described in 1, except to the middle of the court. The post must cut off the angle of the defender with a good drop step. He must reach as far as he can and take the ball directly to the square.

b. *Hook shot.* Post makes a quick drop step, pivots toward the middle of the lane (being sure not to move away from the basket) and goes with a hook shot.

c. *Short jump shot.* The jump shot is taken off both feet, which provides better balance and better rebound position after the shot.

4. Perhaps the toughest time to attack the defender is when he is playing directly behind the post. He can use any of the first five moves, however, he must know where he is and not lose contact with the defender. Additional moves are the front pivot and face-the-basket moves. It is better to pivot on the inside foot towards the middle of the court. Pivoting towards the middle provides a good angle to use for short jump shots. Pivot and face-the-basket moves are

a. Pivot to the middle and take the jump shot.

b. Pivot to the middle, jab and crossover, and shoot power lay-up.

OTHER AREAS OF DEVELOPMENT IN LOW-POST PLAY

Usually we attempt to feed the low post from the wing position, although the wings can also take what is open. If the low post is closely guarded, we flash the weakside post to the foul line area. As soon as the post receives the ball in the high-post area, he looks into the low post for a potential receiver. The low post should start his move to get open when the ball is in the air from wing to the high post. Two situations to be aware of are

1. If the defender was playing low prior to this pass, the post maintains contact, keeping the defender on his back side. Give a big target and demand the ball from the high post.

2. If the defender was playing on the top side, the post executes a drop step, using his free arm now as his leverage arm to keep the defender pinned and then step to the basket with a good target.

If the post is playing in the low post away from the ball, he expects the perimeter players to bring the ball to his side and should be aware of the following. His defender will sag to the middle of the floor when the ball is located on ballside. As the ball is reversed to the post's side of the floor, he steps up the lane to increase the baseline target area, steps into the defender and opens to the ball—giving a big target.

MOVES AND SHOTS FROM HIGH POST

Since the post positions are interchangeable, both posts should be knowledgeable about certain basic movements and shots. Teach the post men to pivot and face the basket upon receiving the ball. This move puts them in position for a quick move or triple threat position. Teach the following moves:

1. *Front pivot and jab moves.* As explained in Chapter 2, all moves should be performed with no more than one dribble or two dribbles if a drive is attempted. Work on practicing the jab moves with a reverse dribble.

2. *Power slide.* The post uses a side-shuffle step to force his way to the basket. He takes a long step to get his shoulder and foot past the defender, and jumps off both feet for a power lay-up.

In developing the moves and shots from the low- and high-post areas, the following drills are utilized. All drills are performed in a series of five from both sides of the court.

1. Individual Moves

The player stands approximately in the middle of the lane with one foot in front of basket. He tosses the ball with reverse spin into the block area, fakes opposite the pass, and moves to receive the ball with a jump stop. After receiving the ball, the player reacts to an imaginary defense. The sequence of moves and shots are: power move with defender on foul lane side, power move with defender on baseline side, front pivot and bank jump shot with defender behind, and hook shot with defender behind or on baseline side. To practice high-post moves, the player tosses the ball to the side post, moves to receive it and front pivots to face basket. The sequence of moves are: jab and go to basket, jab and crossover, jab and jumper, and power slide.

2. Toss-Back

The use of the Toss-Back speeds up the tempo of post moves and shots, along with developing the fundamentals of good passing accuracy, two-hand overhead pass, and receiving the ball.

A. Fan pass drill. The post men line up on the block away from the Toss-Back. The first post in line makes a two-handed overhead pass into the Toss-Back (located at wing position). He moves across the lane, catches the ball in the low-post area, reverse pivots on his left foot and makes another two-hand overhead pass into a Toss-Back, located in a position that will return ball to lane area. Upon receiving the ball, the post makes a power move and repeats the movement again. If a Toss-Back is not available, two players can return the ball back to the player running the drill.

B. Low-post moves and shot drill. The post men line up as they did in the first drill, but upon receiving the ball from the first Toss-Back, they perform a power move (imaginary defender on baseline and foul line side), front pivot and bank jump shot, and left-hand hook shot. The Toss-Back is then moved to other side and the drill is repeated. To make the drill more gamelike, the next post man in line can follow across the lane and apply defensive pressure foul line side, baseline side or behind to challenge the offense to react with the correct offensive move.

C. High-post moves and shot drill. Toss-Back is placed at the top of the key so that the ball will return at the side post. The post makes a two-hand overhead pass into the Toss-Back, quickly moves to the side post to receive ball, front pivots towards basket and shoots a jump shot or works on the jab moves. A defensive man can also be added to the drill.

DRILLS FOR IMPROVING THE POST PLAYER

Spend five minutes every day developing timing, agility, and coordination. Work players in groups of three or four. Following is a list of some of the drills.

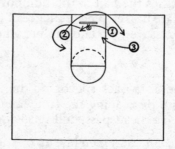

Diagram 4-9

1. *Three-man figure-eight tip drill.* Three players line up as illustrated in Diagram 4-9. Player 01 passes the ball off the backboard to 02 and moves behind 01. Player 02 jumps up, catches ball, and passes ball back off backboard to 03 and moves behind 01. Player 03 continues drill.

2. *Pickups.* This drill involves one player and two balls located on the blocks on each side of the lane and lasts for 30 seconds. The drill starts when the player picks up one of the balls and shoots a lay-up. He then picks up the other ball and shoots another lay-up. The other two players retrieve the balls and place them back on the blocks. The same player continues for the length of time.

3. *Superman drill.* The drill consists of rebounding side by side, back and forth across the lane. The ball is tossed over the goal off the backboard. The player sprints to catch the ball outside the foul line. The drill continues for 30 seconds.

5

Coaching Two- and Three-Man Situations for the

DOUBLE POST

Offense

The individual fundamentals presented in Chapters 2, 3 and 4 were to teach players how to move with and without the basketball in their respective positions. Players must learn to coordinate their individual movements into a pattern of play that will contribute to the team effort. To do this they must be drilled in two- and three-man situations. After mastery of these situations, Chapters 6, 7 and 8 will develop these movements into a smooth and organized offense.

TWO-MAN SITUATIONS

The basic maneuvers of the Double Post Offense are practiced with all players, regardless of position. The two-man situations involve the point with wing, point with post, and wing with post.

The situations are:

1. Give-and-go
2. Backdoor
3. Pass and screen ball
4. Weakside play
5. Single cuts off the post
6. Go behind

At first, teach all of the two-man situations without defense on both sides of the court; then run them against defensive pressure. The

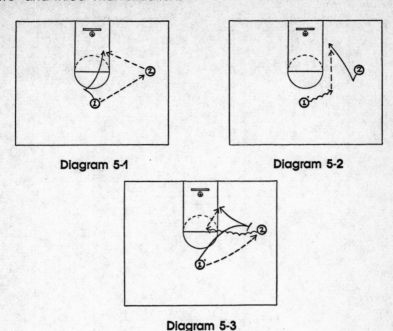

Diagram 5-1   Diagram 5-2

Diagram 5-3

players must be able to read the defense and make the correct maneuvers.

Give-and-go. (Diagram 5-1). The point, 01, passes to the wing, 02, who has made a fake before receiving the ball. 02 squares up at the basket. At the same time, 01 sets up his man by taking two steps to his left, planting his left foot, and cutting directly to the basket over the top of his defender, and extending his left hand for a pass from 02. 02 follows the pass, rebounds the shot, dribbles out of the lane area, passes to the next player in line, and moves to the end of the line.

Backdoor (Diagram 5-2). The wing, 02, takes two steps toward the point, 01, plants his outside foot and makes a direct cut to the basket with his right hand out for a target. The point dribbles toward the wing position, bounce passes to 02, follows the pass, moves to rebound the shot, and passes to the next player in line.

Pass and screen ball (Diagram 5-3). The point passes to the wing, who made a fake before receiving the ball. 01 screens 02's defensive man. 02 dribbles off the screen with his left hand, looking for a jump

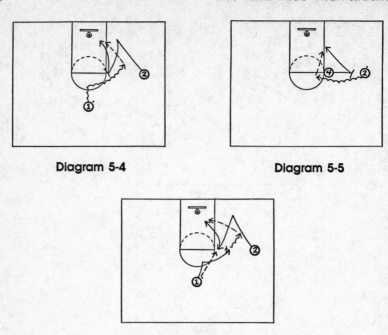

Diagram 5-4   Diagram 5-5

Diagram 5-6

shot or a pass to 01, who reverse pivots toward the basket after the screen. If 02 shoots, 01 rebounds; but if 01 shoots, 02 rebounds. Pass and screen ball should never be run against a defense that is double-teaming.

Screen-and-roll (Diagram 5-4). Wing, 02, breaks to the block on his side of court, plants his right foot, pivots, sprints up the foul line to the side post position, and sets a screen. Point, 01, is dribbling to his left, making a change of direction move, and rubs off 02's screen. As 01 dribbles past 02, 02 pivots on his right foot, swings his left arm and leg around toward the basket, and extends the left hand for a target. 01 has the option of shooting a jump shot or passing to 02 for a lay-up. Practice the screen-and-roll between the post and wing, as illustrated in Diagram 5-5. A point has to be made to the player rolling to the basket. He must always turn and face the ball. The player not attempting the shot rebounds and passes to the next player.

Weakside play (Diagram 5-6). The two-man weakside play is one of the toughest plays in basketball. Wing, 02, breaks to the blocks and moves to the side post but instead of setting a screen as in the pick-and-roll he receives a pass from 01. After 01 passes ball to 02, he takes two steps away from the direction of the pass, plants his left foot and cuts off 02. The following options are available: (1) 02 can drive or shoot a jump shot; (2) 02 can pass to 01, who drives to the basket and shoots a jump shot; or passes back to 02, rolling to the basket.

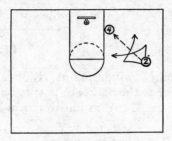

Diagram 5-7

Single cuts off post (Diagram 5-7). This two-man situation is similar to the weakside play, except for the angle from which it develops. The wing, 02, passes to post, 04, in the low-post area. After 02 makes the pass, he takes his defensive man several steps away from the direction toward which he intends to cut. The following options are available: (1) 02 attempts to rub his defender off 04 for a jump shot or driving lay-up; and (2) 04 can make a power move if X4 leans in the direction of 02's cut off the post.

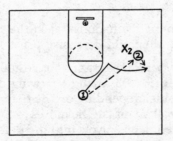

Diagram 5-8

Go behind (Diagram 5-8). Point, 01, passes to wing, 02, and moves to a position that almost screens X2, and then cuts behind 02 for a

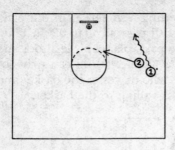

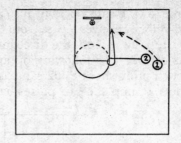

Diagram 5-8A   Diagram 5-8B

return pass. 01 has the following options: (1) 01 can shoot a jump shot over 02; (2) 01 can drive to the basket or pass to 02 (Diagram 5-8A); or (3) 02 can post up (using L cut) as illustrated in Diagram 5-8B.

THREE-MAN SITUATIONS

The three-man situations involve movements of the point, wing, and post working together. These situations are the backbone of the offense. Spend time in developing this area of play.

The situations are:

1. Pass and screen opposite
2. Split the post
3. Post
4. Clear
5. High-post rub

As with the two-man situations, teach the three-man situations without defense first, then add defensive players.

Pass and screen opposite (Diagram 5-9). Post, 01, passes to 02, then moves to set a screen for 03 at the left wing position. 03 can cut baseline or foul line side, depending on the defender's position. If 03 does not receive the ball on his cut, he moves to the ballside corner. 01, after setting the screen, front pivots into the defender and rolls back in the direction of the ball for a pass from 02 for a jump shot. Even if 01 does not receive the ball immediately, he fills the point area to keep the floor balanced and protect the defensive basket.

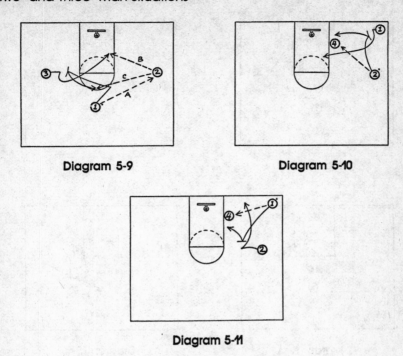

Diagram 5-9   Diagram 5-10

Diagram 5-11

Split the post (Diagrams 5-10 and 5-11). This is one of the strongest three-man plays in the offense. The point, 01, has already passed to 02 and cut to the ballside corner. 04 positions himself to receive the pass from 02. After 02 passes to 04, he screens 01 in the corner. The following options are: (1) 04 can make a move to the basket; (2) 01 can set his defender up for 02's screen, move as close to 04 as possible for a pass for a jump shot; and, (3) 04 can pass to 02, rolling off the screen set for 01. Diagram 5-10 illustrates the split when 01 passes to 04 and screens for 02. The following options are available: (1) 04 can make a move to the basket; (2) 02 can cut off 01's screen, move as close to 04 for a pass for a jump shot; and (3) 04 can pass to 01, rolling off the screen set for 02.

Post (Diagrams 5-12 and 5-13). The point, 01, calls "post" and 04 moves to the high side post. 01 passes the ball to 04. At the same time, 02 steps towards the point area and cuts backdoor for a possible pass from 04. After 01 makes the pass to 04, he steps away from the

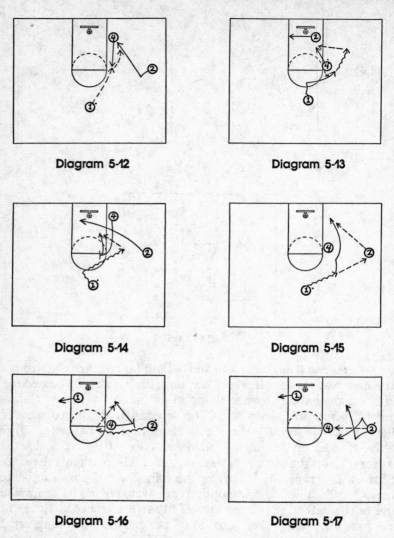

Diagram 5-12

Diagram 5-13

Diagram 5-14

Diagram 5-15

Diagram 5-16

Diagram 5-17

direction of the pass and cuts off 04 for a flip pass. This situation continues like the two-man weakside play.

Clear (Diagram 5-14). The point, 01, calls "clear," 04 moves to the high side post and then sets a screen. 02 clears to the other side of court. 01 dribbles to his left, makes a change of direction and moves off to 04's screen. The situation continues like the pick-and-roll.

High-post rub (Diagrams 5-15 and 5-16). Post, 04, moves to the high side post. 01 dribbles toward the wing area, passes to 02 and cuts off the screen set by 04. If 01 is open, 02 passes to him for lay-up. If 01 is not open, he continues across the lane to the weakside. 02 calls for a screen from 04, who screens for 02 and a pick-and-roll is run (Diagram 5-16). 02 can pass to 04 and cut off him (Diagram 5-17).

If the players have mastered the two- and three-man situations, then proceed to teach the Double Post Offense as a five-man unit.

6

The
DOUBLE POST
Strongside Series

The Double Post strongside series is patterned after Fred (Tex) Winter's Triple Post Offense to develop a strong inside game for two post men, and produce scoring opportunities for the perimeter players against man-to-man defense. The series is two offenses in one—the posts play one offense; the perimeter plays another. The only time they interact is when a perimeter player passes to a post or a post screens a perimeter player. This series forces the defense to keep the ball out of the post area.

The strong side of the court is determined when the point cuts to the corner on the ballside, leaving three players on one side, and the weak side where two players are located. (The right side is the strong side and the left is the weak side.)

In preparing the strong side, this chapter shows how to set the series, the possible options available in the series, and what to do when the option is not available or the play does not work. It also illustrates how to maintain floor balance, and how quickly this series develops into a continuity. The preceding chapters have developed the fundamentals on which this series is founded. By mastering these fundamentals, the players learn to react to the defense and not just think through the movements.

BASIC PATTERN

The basic pattern of the strongside series is initiated when the point man, 01, passes to wing, 02, and makes a cut to the corner on ballside to form a strongside triangle. The onside post man, 04,

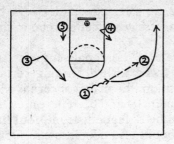

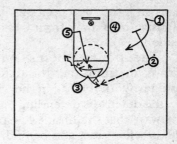

Diagram 6-1   **Diagram 6-2**

positions himself on the block to receive a possible pass from the wing. The post man on the weakside, 05, moves halfway up the lane. The weakside wing, 03, moves to the point area. These movements are shown in Diagram 6-1. If wing, 02, cannot pass to the post area, the ball is passed to weakside wing, 03, at the point, and the weakside game starts (Diagram 6-2).

FORMING THE STRONGSIDE TRIANGLE

The basic pattern of the strongside series is very simple. To make it more difficult on the defense, there are five ways to form the strongside triangle and six formations from which to work. The point, 01, after passing to either wing, 02 or 03, can make any of the four following cuts.

1. Sideline cut (Diagram 1-8)
2. Straight cut (Diagram 1-8)
3. Deep cut (Diagram 1-8)
4. Pass and screen the opposite wing

In the fifth method of forming the strongside triangle, the point dribbles over the wing position and the wing slides to the corner.

OPTIONS FROM THE WING'S POSITION

The end result of the point, 01, passing to wing, 02, and cutting to the corner is shown in Diagram 6-1. The weakside wing, 03, has moved to the point area, while the onside post, 04, positions himself on the block. The weakside post, 05, moves halfway up the lane. The weakside post, 05, positions halfway up the lane and clears his defensive man away from 04's area and creates a better rebounding position.

The strongside formation illustrates a positional setup for the offense, meaning that the defense is faced with defending certain positions. With the ball in the wing position, the main concern is with how the defense is defending our post men, 04 and 05. There are only four ways that the onside low post can be defended: front, foul line side, baseline side, and behind. You should also take into consideration how the weakside post is being defended, and whether the defensive player is helping out. This formation creates situations for getting the ball inside, providing strong rebounding position, and encouraging away-from-the-ball movement.

Option 1: Jump shot or drive the lane

If wing, 02, feels he can shoot a jump shot and score, he has that option. It is usually not in the best interests of the offense for the wing to shoot too often. Post, 05, would rebound the weak side. Post, 04, would have middle responsibility while point, 01, in corner would rebound strong side. Wing, 02, would follow his post, and 03 would defend against a possible fast break.

If wing, 02, feels that he can beat his man one-on-one, he drives to his left to the lane area for a jump shot or a possible pass to 05 or 03, depending on how the defense reacts to his move. If 05's defensive man attempts to pick up 02, 02 can pass to 05 for a power shot under the basket.

The drive by 02 places the players in an unusual position on the weak side if the defense covers successfully. If 02 does drive and a shot does not develop, he must get the ball to 03. The two ways 02 can get the ball to 03 are: (1) pass the ball directly to him; and (2) dribble the ball to 03 and hand it to him.

If 02 completes the pass to 03 on the weak side, 03 and 05 would run a pick-and-roll (two-man weakside play) or, 03 passes to 01 for a jump shot, as illustrated in Diagram 6-3. Anytime 02 passes the ball, he screens down on 01's man, except when he passes to 01 in the corner. In this case, 02 can hold his position or screen the weakside wing, 03, and exchange positions.

If 02 continues his dribble towards 03 on the weakside, 03 cuts off 02 for a handoff. Wing, 03, can drive down the middle of the lane for a jump shot or pass to either 05 or 04 if their defensive man

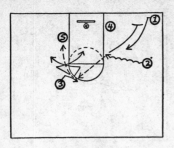

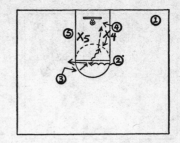

Diagram 6-3   Diagram 6-4

attempts to stop him (Diagram 6-4). 01 moves to point area for defensive coverage if 03 drives the lane. If 03 is successfully stopped at the foul line, he passes to 01 and 02 at the wing area and starts the series over again.

The major functions of the strongside wing are to pass and screen. Let us now consider a pass to the post and the options available.

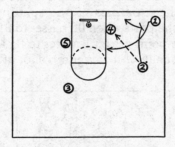

Diagram 6-5

Option 2: Pass to the pivot and split the post

If the wing, 02, passes to the onside low post, 04, which is the basic play of the strongside series, the post's first option is to attempt a one-on-one if he feels he can beat his man. While the post is trying to score, the wing, 02, screens 01 in the corner, and they execute a wing-guard split (Diagram 6-5). Anytime the wing passes to the post, he screens baseline guard. The post, 04, can hand off to 01 or 02. If post, 04, cannot shoot or pass to 01 or 02, it is 03's responsibility to get open so that he can gain possession of the ball and the offense can continue.

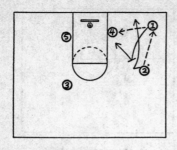

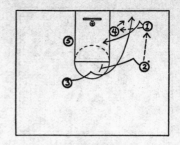

Diagram 6-6   Diagram 6-7

Option 3: Pass to the corner and split the post

If the wing, 02, passes to the guard, 01, in the corner, 01 has the option of passing to the post, 04, and executing a guard-wing split as illustrated in Diagram 6-6. 01, upon receiving the ball, must immediately look to pass to post, 04, before 04's defensive man can shift from foul line side to baseline side. 01, the passer, becomes the screener as he screens 02, If 04 does not have the opportunity to shoot, he hands off to 02 or 01. Again, it is 03's responsibility to get open if 04 cannot shoot or pass to the splitting players. Another method for splitting the posts when 02 passes to 01 in the corner is for 02 to screen 03 at the point area. 01 passes to 04 and sets a screen on 03 (Diagram 6-7). Usually 03 has a jump shot after receiving a pass from 04.

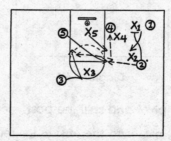

Diagram 6-8

Option 4: Pass to weakside post flashing high

If 05's defensive man is sagging in the lane to help 04's defensive man prevent the pass to low post, or if the defense is denying 03 the ball at the point, then the weakside post, 05, flashes to the high post to counter this pressure. Wing, 02, has the option to pass to 05 and screen 01. 05 has the following options (Diagram 6-8):

1. Shoot a jump shot.
2. Pass to 04 who has pinned his man on his backside at the low post.
3. Pass to 01, coming off 02's screen.
4. Pass to 03, cutting backdoor.

Wing, 02, also has the option to lob pass to post, 04, if 05's defensive man denies the pass from 02 to 05.

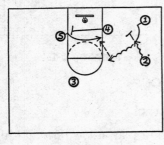

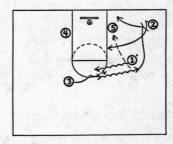

| Diagram 6-9 | Diagram 6-10 |

Option 5: Dribble weave

If the wing cannot pass the ball inside because of sagging defense, the weave movement provides a good means to move the ball closer to the basket. Diagram 6-9 illustrates wing, 02, dribbling to the inside of 01. 02 comes to a jump stop and hands off to 01. The post area becomes dangerous again because the defense has to pick up their man while the ball is being dribbled around the perimeter. The player guarding the post will be on the wrong side of the post, especially if 04 screens for 05. 01's first option is to drive over the top of the screen toward the basket for a shot. He could pass to 05, cutting off 04's screen for the second option. In his third option, he can continue dribbling to the inside of 03, who can pass to 04 and start the strongside series as shown in Diagram 6-10. Occasionally, 03 might dribble down the lane for a lay-up, or a pass to 04 or 05.

The wing, 02, can dribble to the inside of 03 (Diagram 6-12). 02 comes to a jump stop and hands off to 03, who has several options. The first is to drive over the top of the screen toward the basket to shoot or pass off to 04 or 05, if their defensive men pick him up. 03 can continue dribbling to the inside of 01, who has the same options as illustrated in Diagram 6-9. 01 can start the strongside series again from the wing position.

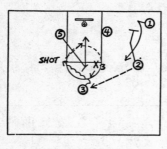

Diagram 6-11   Diagram 6-12

WEAKSIDE OPTIONS

Option 1: Wing passes to point for jump shot

The defense is trying to stop the post play at low post and high post by sagging into the lane area and jamming the basket area. Wing, 02, passes to the weakside wing, 03, for a jump shot at the top of the key.

Option 2: Weakside pick-and-roll

If the weakside wing, 03, is unable to shoot from the point area, this keys the start of the weakside options, the first of which is a weakside pick-and-roll. Anytime wing, 02, passes, he screens 01 in the corner. Weakside post, 05, positioning himself halfway up the lane, screens 03's defensive man who has charged 03 to take away his shot (Diagram 6-11). If 03 does not have a shot or cannot pass to 05, rolling down the lane, he passes back out to 01, and the offense starts again.

Option 3: Weakside high-post rub

Diagram 6-12 illustrates the high-post rub between 03 and 05. This offers a variety of options. Weakside post, 05, breaks to the side post. 03 passes to 05 and cuts off 05. 05 can shoot a jump shot, drive the lane or hand off to 03. 03 can shoot or pass to 05, rolling down the

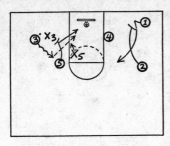 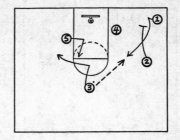

Diagram 6-13   **Diagram 6-14**

lane, or pass to 01, cutting off of 02's screen.

Occasionally after 03 receives the handoff from 05, X3 prevents the drive to the basket, and 05 is defensed correctly by X5. 03 can reverse dribble and receive a screen from 05 and execute a pick-and-roll (Diagram 6-13). This option is called a weakside reverse dribble pick-and-roll. 03 has the option of shooting a jump shot, passing to 05 rolling down the lane, passing to 01 cutting off of 02's screen, or dribble weaving with 01. If 05 is overplayed, he cuts backdoor for a pass from 03.

Option 4: Pass to baseline guard, on strong side

If the defense overreacts to the weakside options, 03 fakes the high-post rub and passes to 01, cutting off 02's screen for a jump shot (Diagram 6-14). If 01 does not shoot, he can dribble out and start the offense again.

Option 5: Shuffle cut

The shuffle cut provides a set play to use in the beginning and end of each quarter. It is used whenever you want a lay-up, or to maintain ball control. The shuffle is keyed by a hand or verbal signal, depending upon your preference, and we have used both.

Wing, 02, passes to 03 at the top of the key; 01 moves several steps towards lane; 04 steps up and sets a screen for 02; 05 breaks from his position halfway up the lane to the left wing area where he receives a pass from 03 (Diagram 6-15).

In Diagram 6-16, 02 fakes toward baseline, drives his defensive man into 04, and cuts to the basket for the first option. 03 cuts behind 02 as near to 05 as possible. 04 then breaks toward the ball for the

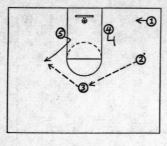

Diagram 6-15   **Diagram 6-16**

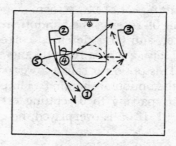

Diagram 6-17

second option to the medium post. The third option is 01 at the top of the key after being screened by 03. If players 02, 04, and 01, upon receiving the ball, have a shot they will take it. If the ball is passed out to 01, and 01 does not shoot, he passes the ball to 03 to continue the shuffle action (Diagram 6-17).

After 03 receives the ball from 01, he has three options. The first option of 03's is to pass to 05, who fakes toward the baseline, drives his man into 04, and cuts to the basket. 01 cuts behind 05 as near to 04 as possible. The second option is 04 breaking toward the ball to medium post. 02 breaks to top of the key after being screened by 01. 03 can pass to any of the three cutters. The shuffle continues until a shot is taken.

Option 6: Give-and-go for post

If the defensive post men are not very mobile, or can not play good defense away from the basket, a give-and-go for one of the posts is set up. 03 screens down for 05 to break to the point area and receives a pass from 02. 05 immediately passes to 03 rolling off the

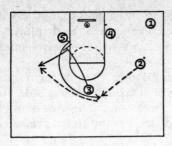
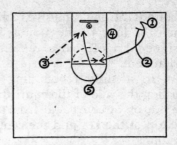

Diagram 6-18   Diagram 6-19

screen to the wing area (Diagram 6-18). Occasionally a switch will take place. After 05 passes to 03, he takes several steps away from the ball, plants his right foot and cuts hard to the basket for a pass from 03 (Diagram 6-19). If a mismatch occurs, 05 can post up or can make a single cut off the post. 03 can also pass to 01.

COMBINATION MOVES

To increase the chances of getting the ball inside and add movement to the offense, you can teach three combination moves to the post men. These moves were described in Chapter 4. The combination moves make it very hard for the defensive men to play honestly on your post. Whenever the ball is passed to the wing, the onside post has four options:

1. Position himself on the ballside.
2. Fan (Diagram 4-14).
3. Roll (Diagram 4-15).
4. Away (Diagram 4-16).

The coordination of the movements between the point and the post is consistent with the rules laid out in Chapter 1. The point makes the first cut and the onside post makes the second cut. The offense continues as outlined in this chapter.

OFFENSIVE REBOUND AND DEFENSIVE RESPONSIBILITIES

Successful offensive teams secure 40 to 45% of their own total rebounds. Strong offensive rebounding can win games that otherwise would be lost. In the Double Post offensive system, each player is assigned an offensive rebounding position or defensive safety assignment.

To identify rebounding positions, divide the court in half, labeling the side of the court the ball is shot from as strong side and the side of the court away from the ball as weak side. The area between the top of the key and the center jump circle is the defensive safety position.

The basic method used in this offensive rebounding is to send three-and-a-half players to cover the basket and assign one-and-a-half players as defensive safeties. As we proceed through the offense, rebounding responsibilities and safety assignments illustrate that this is a strong rebounding offense.

Offensive Rebounding Rules

1. The onside post man is responsible for rebounding ballside low-post area.
2. The weakside post man rebounds the weakside low-post area.
3. Onside wing has middle rebounding responsibility on all shots.
4. Weakside wing is the defensive safety.
5. The point man has high rebound responsibility around the foul line.

On a shot by wing, 02, the rebound assignments are: 05 fills the weakside position, 04 fills ballside low-post position, 02 fills middle position, 01 fills high rebound position, and 03 the defensive safety.

On a shot by 01 in the corner: 05 fills the weakside position, 04 fills ballside position, 02 fills middle area, 01 has the option of following his shot or moving to the key area, and 03 is the defensive safety.

The rebounding assignments are the same when the ball is passed to 04, and 02 and 01 split. It makes no difference whether the shot is taken by 04 in the post area, 02 at the baseline, or 01 in the wing area.

The rebound assignments would also be the same if 02 passes to 03 at the top of the key for a shot.

The rebound assignments when 02 passes to 05 flashing to high-post are: 05 fills weak side, 04 fills ballside position, 02 fills middle position, 03 fills high rebounding area, and 01 is the defensive safety.

When a shot is taken by 03 while executing the weakside options, the rebound assignments are: 04 fills low-post weak side, 05 fills low-post ballside, 03 fills middle rebound position, and 01 fills high rebound position, and 02 becomes the defensive safety.

If 01 takes the shot off a pass from 05 when executing the weakside option, 05 and 04 rebound in the low positions, 02 fills middle position, 01 moves to high rebound area, and 03 is the defensive safety.

Each coach must decide how to assign players responsibilities based on the talents and abilities of his particular team.

STRONGSIDE SERIES FROM SIX OTHER FORMATIONS

This section demonstrates how to get from the six basic formations into the strongside formation (Diagram 6-1). (The strongside series from a 1-2-2 set has already been explained in great detail and needs no further discussion.)

The personnel of a team changes each year, but the fundamentals remain the same. In order to use the physical qualities and abilities of the players on a year-to-year and a game-to-game basis, the seven alignments allow us to utilize these attributes to develop a versatile offense against teams that play a variety of defenses.

Every team can be beaten. By using a specific alignment and emphasizing specific situations based on a comparison of the opponents' abilities, a game plan can be formulated to contrast their styles.

From a 1-3-1 alignment (Diagram 1-2), the offense starts differently depending upon the side from which the entry pass is made. If the entry pass is made to the side of the high post, the point, 01, cuts behind post, 04, before moving to the corner. The onside post, 04, can slide down the lane to receive a pass from 02 or make any one of the three combination moves. The weakside post, 05, moves halfway up the lane, and the weakside wing, 03, moves to the point area.

If the point, 01, makes the entry pass to wing, 03, on the low-post side, he can make a straight cut to the corner, or screen the opposite wing so the ball can be passed to low post, 05. If 01 cuts to the corner, the onside post is a strong offensive maneuver. If 01 screens opposite wing, 02, it means that the ball can be gotten to the low post without any problems.

Diagram 1-3 represents the 1-4 high alignment. This alignment is used when your players are quicker than the opponents. The point, 01, can rub his defensive player off the post men, 04 and 05, after a pass to the wings, 02 or 03. The post men can use their quickness in the combination moves from the high-post area. Passing and screening to the opposite wing yields an opportunity to post up a wing with the post men high. If the wing does not receive the ball low, he can move to the corner and form the strongside triangle.

From the 1-4 low alignment (Diagram 1-4), the point, 01, dribbles to the wing area, and wings, 02 and 03, exchange positions to form the strongside triangle. Wing, 02, moves to the point for balance. The posts, 04 and 05, execute any one of the three combination moves.

The stack alignments are illustrated in Diagrams 1-5 and 1-6. The strongside series is run in the same manner as in the 1-2-2 and 1-3-1 alignments. The advantage is that the wings, 02 and 03, can break from behind the stack for a quick pass and jump shot, cross and proceed to opposite wings or screen for each other before moving to the wing area to receive a pass from the point. The stack alignments are good for release moves to initiate the offense.

Diagram 1-7 illustrates the unbalanced stack. This alignment offers the point, 01, and wing, 02, an opportunity to run two-man plays before the strongside triangle is formed. Also, a triple screen can be set to initiate the series if point, 01, screens wing, 03. 03 can then cut off of 01's screen and behind the double screen set by the posts, 04 and 05. If 03 does not receive the ball, he can move to the corner and one of the posts can cut to ballside to form the strongside triangle. Point, 01, moves to the top of the key for balance.

The strongside series is a positional offense in that you create situations to get the ball inside, provide strong rebounding position and encourage away-from-the-ball movement.

Now briefly, here is a summary of the options of the strongside series:

1. Strongside wing's options
    a. Jump shot or drive the lane
    b. Pass to the pivot and split the post
    c. Pass to the corner

      d. Pass to weakside post flashing high
      e. Dribble weave

2. Weakside options
      a. Weakside wing shoots jump shot
      b. Pick-and-roll
      c. High-post rub
      d. Pass to baseline guard
      e. Shuffle cut

7
Weakside Series for the
DOUBLE POST
Offense

The weakside series gives the wings scoring opportunities not available from the strongside series. This series emphasizes two-man situations with continual motion until a shot develops. As in the strongside series, emphasis is placed on passing to the post—this series also provides us with these opportunities.

The series is keyed by the point's cut over the onside post and movement away from the ball to the weakside; hence, the name, weakside series.

Use this dimension of the offense if your wings are good jump shooters off a screen. If your players are proficient at the two-man situations of give-and-go, pick-and-roll, and posting up, this is the offensive series for you to use.

ENTRY TO WEAKSIDE SERIES—PASS AND CUT

The series is initiated when point, 01, dribbles with short shuffling steps until he reaches side foul line extended. The dribbling movement helps set the rub off. He then passes to wing, 02. The onside post, 04, moves to the side of the foul line and sets a screen. Point, 01, takes a step with his left foot and attempts to rub his man off the screen set by post, 04. 02 should pass the ball to him (Diagram 7-1). 01 should attempt a lay-up or a short jump shot, depending on the type of defensive coverage he encounters. This is a strong cut if your point guard has good inside moves.

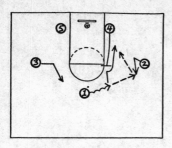 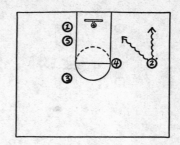

Diagram 7-1   **Diagram 7-2**

OPTIONS FROM THE WING POSITION

After point, 01, passes to wing, 02, and cuts off screen set by outside post, 04, and does not receive a pass from 02, he moves to stack behind the weakside post, 05. The weakside wing, 03, moves to the side foul line extended. These movements are shown in Diagram 7-2. Wing, 02, has the following options.

Option 1: Drive baseline

After 02 receives the ball, he squares up at the basket. If he cannot pass to 01 cutting for the basket, he jab steps towards the baseline. If his defensive man does not honor his fake, he drives baseline for a lay-up or jump shot (Diagram 7-2). If the defensive man honors his fake, it sets him up for a screen, the next option.

Option 2: Post-wing pick-and-roll

Onside post, 04, reads 02's offensive movement, and then moves to screen 02's defensive man. 02 and 04 run a pick-and-roll. 02 drives left off 04's screen. He can drive for a lay-up or shoot a jump shot. If a switch occurs between 04's defensive man and 02's defensive man, 04 rolls towards the basket for a possible pass (Diagram 7-3).

If a shot does not develop, 02 must continue the offense by getting the ball to the weak side by a dribble exchange with 03, a pass to 03, or pass to 01 after a screen down by 03.

If 02 continues his dribble towards 03 on the weak side, 03 cuts off 02 for a handoff. 03 can drive down the lane for a lay-up or jump

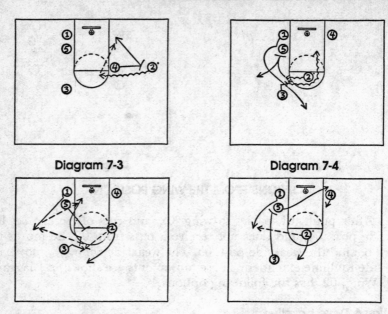

Diagram 7-3   **Diagram 7-4**

Diagram 7-5   **Diagram 7-6**

shot. If 04 or 05's defensive man drops off to cover 03, he passes to the free teammate. After the hand off, 02 screens down on 01, who moves to the point for court balance (Diagram 7-4). If 03 is unable to shoot, he passes back out to 01 and continues the series on the left side of the floor. Occasionally, 03 will dribble to the opposite wing position and pass to 01, who in turn passes to 02 and the offense continues.

If wing, 02, is successfully defended and forced to pick up his dribble, he passes to 03 who tries to receive the ball side lane extended. 03 passes to 01, breaking to the wing area foul line extended. Post, 05, moves to the high side post to set a screen. 03 takes a step to his right, attempts to rub his man off 05's screen and looks for a return pass from 01 (Diagram 7-5).

If wing, 02, cannot pass to 03 because 03 is being overplayed, 03 screens down on 01, stacked with 05, in the low-post area. 01 breaks off 03's screen to the wing area, looking for a pass from 02. 01's first option is a jump shot or a drive (Diagram 7-6). 03 moves across the lane and stacks behind 04. 02 moves to the top of the key for offensive balance. If 01 is unable to shoot or pass to 05 posting up, 05 enters into the play by setting a screen on 01. The screen is set on the baseline side of 01's defensive man. 01 makes a jab step toward the foul line to set his defensive man up, and then dribbles off the screen looking for a shot or a pass to 05 rolling down the lane.

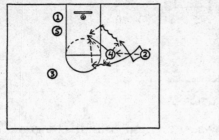

Diagram 7-7　　　　　　　　　　　Diagram 7-8

Option 3: Give-and-go with post

Diagram 7-7 illustrates a give-and-go with post. Here wing, 02, passes to post, 04, steps towards point area and then cuts backdoor or steps towards baseline and cuts over the top of 04. Post, 04, passes the ball to 02 for a shot or goes one-on-one with his defensive man after 02 clears the lane. Wing, 03, moves to key area for offensive balance. When 02 cuts behind 04 and receives a handoff, he can shoot or pass to 04 rolling down the lane.

Option 4: Split

Diagram 7-8 shows a high-post split with wing, 02, and weakside wing, 03. When wing, 02, passes to post, 04, he cuts behind 04 and sets a screen on 03's defensive man. 03 cuts off 02's screen and receives a pass from 04. He has the option of shooting a jump shot or passing to 04 rolling down the lane. 02 stays at the point for offensive balance.

COMBINATION MOVES

To increase the chances of getting the ball to the post men, as in the strongside series, we use the three combination moves of fan, roll, and away. This keeps the post movements consistent with the offensive teachings. The post moves should be spontaneous. When the ball is in the wing position, the onside post has four options: (1) position himself on the ballside, (2) fan, (3) roll, and (4) away.

It should also be noted that the post men have the option to cut

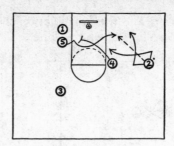

Diagram 7-9

to receive the ball in the low-post area on ballside. Diagram 7-9 illustrates the movement of post, 05, to the low-post area after receiving a pass from wing, 02. 05 has the following options: make a power move, pass to 02 cutting off of him, or pass to 03 if neither of the above options are available. An alternative option is to have post, 05, screen wing, 02. 02 can drive baseline for a lay-up, jump shot or a pass to 05 rolling down the lane.

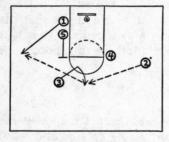

Diagram 7-10

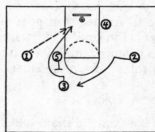

Diagram 7-11

REVERSING OPTIONS

Our reversing options are initiated when wing, 02, sees that the onside options are not available. For wing, 03, the first move to make is a "V" cut to receive the ball at the top of the key as shown in Diagram 7-10. Point, 01, moves behind the stack to the wing area for a pass from 03. 03 cuts off the screen for a possible pass from 01 (Diagram 7-11). If 03 does not receive a pass from 01, he proceeds across the lane and stacks behind post, 04, who has moved back down the lane. 01 now has all the options that were available to 02 on the right side of the court. Usually the offense does not get that far before a shot is taken, but players should be aware of the continuity in case they run across a strong defensive team.

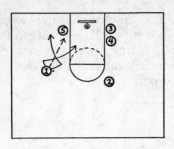

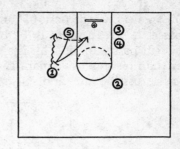

Diagram 7-12   **Diagram 7-13**

If wing, 02, cannot pass to wing, 03, because of defensive pressure, he screens down on point, 01, as previously illustrated in Diagram 7-6. 01's first option is to shoot a jump shot or drive down the lane. His second option is to pass to post, 05, and make a solo cut (Diagram 7-12). 01's third option is for post, 05, to run a pick-and-roll (Diagram 7-13). Wing, 02, provides offensive balance.

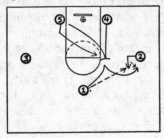

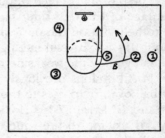

Diagram 7-14   **Diagram 7-15**

ALTERNATE ENTRIES TO THE WEAKSIDE SERIES

To provide variety to the series, we inserted two options for the point: (1) pass and go behind, (2) pass and screen opposite. Both options change the timing of the offense, allowing your players to catch the defense off guard.

The go behind allows you to post up your wings, start the series from a different movement, and give the point man the ball with a dribble. Instead of point, 01, cutting off 04's screen after passing to wing, 02, he cuts behind 02 for a return pass as illustrated in Diagram 7-14. When post, 04, sees the point going behind 02, he automatically exchanges with post, 05. The weakside wing, 03, moves to the side line extended.

Diagram 7-15 shows the two possible routes of wing, 02. In route

A, 02 breaks towards post, 05, and cuts in front of him to the basket. 01 passes to 02. In route B, 02 breaks in front of 05 and cuts to the basket. 01 passes to 02. This is an especially strong play if the wing is taller than his defensive man. If the wing cannot receive the ball, he moves across the lane and stacks behind post, 04.

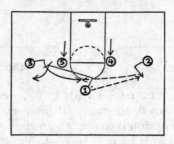

Diagram 7-16

The pass and screen opposite by the point guard is used to take advantage of the weakside wing's (03) defensive man sagging in the lane to help out on the post-wing pick-and-roll, which occurs earlier without 01's cut. By eliminating the point guard's cut over 04's screen and taking away the weakside help, wing, 02, can drive baseline one-on-one. All options previously discussed can be used. If 02 wants to turn ball over, he passes to the weakside wing, 03, at the point for a jump shot (Diagram 7-16). If 03 cannot shoot a jump shot, he passes to point, 01, rolling to the wing area after the screen. 03 cuts off 05's screen looking for a return pass. The offense proceeds as previously discussed.

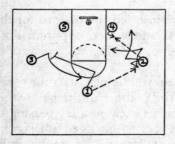

Diagram 7-17

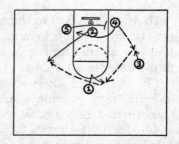

Diagram 7-18

If your post men can continually beat their defensive men, leave the post men low and let the point screen the opposite wing every time. Diagram 7-17 illustrates wing, 02, passing to post, 04, and making a solo cut off the post. Post, 04, will go one-on-one or pass to 02 cutting toward the basket. If 04 cannot shoot or pass to 02 cutting, 03 moves to the wing area, 01 moves back to the point, and 02 moves to the opposite wing as illustrated in Diagram 7-18. 04 passes to 03, who in turn passes to 01, who in turn passes to 02. Wing, 02, can shoot a jump shot, pass to 04 cutting off of 05's screen, or call for 04 to set a screen for a pick-and-roll. After 01 passes to 02, he screens opposite and the movement continues until a shot develops.

REBOUND ASSIGNMENTS

On a shot by 01, the following rebound assignments are made: 01 fills ballside, 05 fills low-post weak side, 04 fills middle position, 02 moves to high rebound position, and 03 moves to the defensive safety.

On a shot by 02 from the wing position, 04 fills ballside low post, 05 fills middle position, 01 fills low-post weak side, 02 can follow his shot or move to high rebound area, and 03 moves to the defensive safety. A drive by 02 is covered the same way.

The rebound coverage from post-wing pick-and-roll with a shot by 02 or 04 is: 05 fills middle position, 01 fills low-post weak side, 04 fills low-post ballside, 02 covers high rebound area, and 03 moves to defensive safety.

The rebound coverage from a shot by 03 off the dribble weave would be as follows: 04 fills ballside low post, 05 fills weakside low post, 03 follows shot and covers the middle position, 02 moves to the high rebound area, and 01 is the defensive safety.

On a shot by 01 or 05 on a weakside pick-and-roll, the rebound coverage is: 04 fills middle rebound coverage, 03 fills low-post weak side, 05 fills low-post ballside, 01 has the option of following his shot or moving to high rebound position, and 02 remains as a defensive safety.

The rebound responsibilities on a give-and-go between the wing and the post are: 04 fills low-post ballside, 02 follows shot or assumes high rebound area, 05 fills middle position, 02 has low-post weak side, and 03 becomes the defensive safety.

On a high-post split with a shot from 03 or 04, the rebound

coverage is: 03 fills low-post ballside, 04 fills high rebound position or follows shot, 05 fills middle position, 01 fills low-post weak side, and 02 becomes the defensive safety.

WEAKSIDE SERIES FROM SIX OTHER FORMATIONS

From a 1-3-1 alignment (Diagram 1-2), the offense starts differently, depending upon from which side the entry pass is made. If the entry pass is made to the side of the high post, 05, before point, 01, rubs his defensive man off the high-post screen, this particular post movement leads to the high-post split illustrated in Diagram 7-8.

If the point, 01, makes the entry pass to the side of the low post, post 05 can move to the high side post to set the screen for 01's cut, or, post, 04, can slide across the lane on the low-post weakside.

Diagram 1-3 represents the 1-4 high alignment. From this alignment the wings have plenty of room for backdoor cuts and putting pressure on the defense. Also, by positioning both post men high, you eliminate weakside defensive help on 01's cut off the high post.

From the 1-4 low alignment (Diagram 1-4) after the point, 01, passes to a wing, the posts, 04 and 05, break and cross to the high side post to set the screen for 01's cut.

The stack alignments are illustrated in Diagrams 1-5 and 1-6. The weakside series is run in the same manner as in the 1-2-2 and 1-3-1 alignments. All movements by wings and posts that were previously discussed can be used to initiate the series.

Diagram 1-7 illustrates the unbalanced stack. After point, 01, passes to a wing, the posts, 04 and 05, have the option for one of them to break high on ballside and the other to stay low on the weak side.

In summary, the options of the weakside series are:

1. Options from the wing position
   a. Drive baseline
   b. Post-wing pick-and-roll
   c. Give-and-go with post
   d. Split

2. Weakside options
   a. Jump shot
   b. High-post rub
   c. Screen down
3. Alternate entries
   a. Pass and go behind
   b. Pass and screen opposite

8

Employing the Post and Clear Series for the
DOUBLE POST
Offense

To be consistent offensively each year, it is important to develop ways of getting the ball in the lane area. The post and clear series helps accomplish this task of getting the ball in the post area. The post series starts with a pass, while the clear series starts with a screen, although both take advantage of two-man situations.

The post series and clear series include some strong offensive concepts:

1. A release against strong pressure man defense

2. One-on-one for post and point

3. Strong two-man situations

4. Continuity

5. Strong rebounding

In both series, it is imperative that the post men find a means of freeing themselves to receive the ball at high side foul lane or to position themselves at the proper angle for a screen on the point. The post men must time their freeing movements for when the point is between the center jump circle and top of key. It is the responsibility of the point to pass to the posts when they are open.

The alignment of the different double post sets aids the post men in freeing themselves for a pass from the point. Along with the alignments, we provide several methods for the post men to free themselves during the game. (These options were discussed in Chapter 4.)

1. Break from the low post (Diagram 4-7).
2. Low-post interchange (Diagram 4-8).
3. X-move (Diagram 4-9).
4. High-low screen (Diagram 4-10).
5. Stack (Diagrams 4-12 and 4-13).

All of the above-mentioned movements end with players positioned in a 1-4 alignment. This clears the area to the basket behind the post men, providing backdoor cuts for the wings against pressure defense.

POST SERIES

Each time your players have the ball, it is desirable to have it passed to one of your posts as he breaks to the side high post; but more often than not, the ball is passed to a wing and another phase of the offense is started.

We have a rule that is mandatory for the post men to follow: Anytime the wing is overplayed and denied the ball, the posts automatically break to the high side post area for a pass from the point.

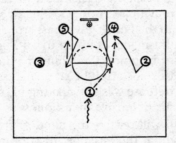

Diagram 8-1

Option 1: Backdoor for onside wing

Diagram 8-1 shows point, 01, crossing the center jump circle and the post men, 04 and 05, breaking to the side high post. It is important for the point man to be aware that the defense will defend this move from the inside out and will very rarely overplay for fear of

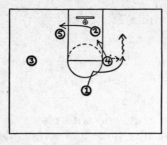

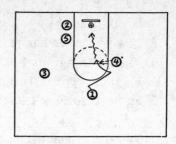

Diagram 8-2   Diagram 8-3

a backdoor cut to the post. The point should make his pass to the post's outside hand, away from his defensive man.

Point, 01, passes to post, 04, and then steps away from the direction of the pass. 02 breaks backdoor to the basket after 04 receives the ball. 04 bounce passes to 02 for a possible lay-up. There is very little defensive help against this backdoor cut, especially with a strong overplay by the defense.

Option 2: Point breaking off post

Diagram 8-2 illustrates the point, 01, breaking off of the post, 04, for a return pass. If the play is run quickly enough, a lay-up will result for 01 driving to the basket. Occasionally, 01 can shoot a jump shot after receiving the return pass from 04. If 04's defensive man switches to cover 01, 04 rolls to the basket for a pass from 01. This move by the defense produces a mismatch between 01 and 04's man.

An alternate cut by point, 01, is illustrated in Diagram 8-3. The point would make this cut after he had successfully completed the outside cut and the defense was anticipating his move. Usually 01 gets a lay-up and keeps his defensive man honest.

Occasionally, 01 will receive the handoff from 04 and be cut off by his defensive man, at the baseline. 01 continues his dribble as 04 moves down to screen his defensive man, as shown in Diagram 8-4 for a pick-and-roll. This can be a very successful play because of the unexpected angle the screen is coming from.

Option 3: Post goes one-on-one

If, upon receiving the ball, 04's defensive man has taken himself out of position by attempting to deny the pass, 04 makes a power slide

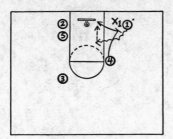

Diagram 8-4

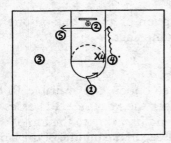

Diagram 8-5

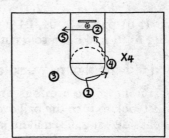

Diagram 8-6

move down the lane for a shot (Diagram 8-5). If 04's defensive man attempts to slow down 01's dribble after he receives the handoff by stepping in front of 01, 04 fakes handoff and power slides down the lane for a lay-up (Diagram 8-6).

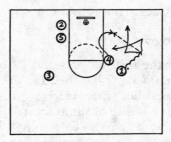

Diagram 8-7

Option 4: Onside pivot post up low

Diagram 8-7 illustrates what happens when 01's dribble gets forced out wide. When this happens, 04 breaks low to post up on the

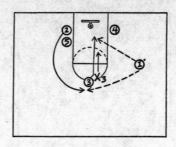

Diagram 8-8

block. If 01 passes to 04, 04 has the option of going one-on-one or passing to 01 making a solo cut for a jump shot.

Option 5: Jump shot by weakside wing

If none of the previously mentioned options are available, 01 or 04 must look to turn the ball over to attack the weak side. 01 passes to the weakside wing, 03, making a V-cut and breaking to the top of the key. Occasionally, 03's defensive man will sag in the middle of the lane, leaving 03 open for a jump shot. If 03 is overplayed on his cut to the top of the key, he immediately breaks backdoor to the basket looking for a pass from 01 (Diagram 8-8). As 03 makes his backdoor cut, 02 moves from behind 05 in the stack to the top of the key for offensive balance and also for a pass from 01 if 03 is not open (Diagram 8-8). If 03 is not open, he moves to stack behind 05, and 02 has the option of shooting a jump shot or driving down the lane.

Option 6: Weakside play

Upon receiving the ball, 03 passes to 02 breaking to the wing area from behind the stack. 02 has the following options available to him: (1) shoot a jump shot upon receiving the ball; (2) drive the middle of the lane for a lay-up or jump shot; (3) drive to the baseline and shoot a jump shot; (4) pass to 05 posting up low, or; (5) 05 can come out to screen 02 for a pick-and-roll (Diagram 8-9). After 03 passes to 02, he screens, so that if 02 needs to continue the offense, 01 can continue it.

The strongest option of the weakside play is a pass from 02 to 05 on the baseline side (Diagram 8-10). 05's defensive man sags in the middle of the lane to help X4, and as the ball is turned over X5 is

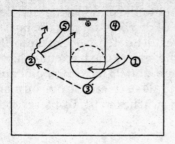

Diagram 8-9

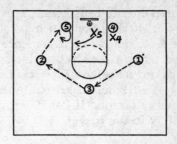

Diagram 8-10

taught to overplay foul line side when the ball is positioned at the wing. So, if 05 positions himself up the lane several feet above the block, and 02 makes a good pass on the baseline, two points may result.

CLEAR SERIES

We have found over the years that this is one of the strongest plays in the offense. The execution of this play is extremely important. If you have an outstanding point man, this is the play to use.

Both post men, 04 and 05, break out from the low-post position to the high side post area after the point dribbles across the center jump circle. Each post man sets a screen and is prepared for the point, 01, to drive his defensive man off him.

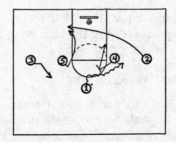

Diagram 8-11

Option 1: Pick-and-roll

Diagram 8-11 illustrates the clear series, starting with a screen.

The point, 01, calls "clear." This indicates to the onside wing that he is to clear to the other side of court when 01 dribbles towards the post on his side. 04 has set a screen. 01 drives his defensive man into 04's screen and passes to 04 rolling down the lane to the basket. 05 moves back down the lane, 02 stacks behind him, and 03 moves to point area.

If 01's defensive man goes behind 04's screen, 01 pulls up and shoots a jumper. If 04's defensive man switches to 01, 01 passes to 04 rolling to the basket.

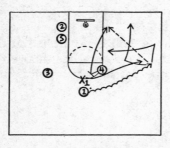

Diagram 8-12

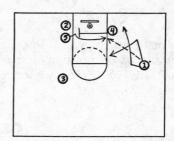

Diagram 8-13

Option 2: Onside pivot posts up low

Diagram 8-12 illustrates what happens when 01's defensive man anticipates the screen and steps out wide to the wing area. Post 04 has rolled low to post up on the block. If 01 passes to 04, 04 has the option of going one-on-one or passing to 01 making a solo cut for a jump shot.

A strong free-lance move for 04 is to move across the lane to screen post, 05. 05, upon receiving the ball, can go one-on-one or pass to 01 making a solo cut (Diagram 8-13).

Option 3: Jump shot by weakside wing

If none of the previously mentioned options are available, 01 or 04 must look to turn the ball over to attack the weak side. 01 passes to the weakside wing, 03, making a V-cut breaking to the top of the key. If 03's man sags in the middle of the lane, 03 shoots a jump shot. If 03 is overplayed on his cut to the top of the key, he immediately cuts backdoor to the basket looking for a pass from 01 (Diagram 8-14). As 03 makes his cut toward the basket, 02 moves from behind 05 in the stack to the top of the key for a pass from 01 if 03 is not open

(Diagram 8-14). If 03 is not open, he moves behind 05 and 02 has the option to shoot a jump shot or drive down the lane.

Option 4: Weakside play

The weakside play is the same as in the post series, as illustrated in Diagram 8-10. 03 passes to 02 breaking to the wing area from behind the stack. 02 has the following options available from there: (1) shoot a jump shot; (2) drive the middle of the lane; (3) drive the baseline for a jump shot; (4) pass to 05 posting up low, and (5) 05 can move out to screen 02 for a pick-and-roll. After 03 passes to 02, he screens 01, so if 02 needs to continue the offense, 01 can continue it.

Both the post and clear series have been successful in producing high percentage shots. When a basket is needed in close games, the post and clear series are used as the primary offense.

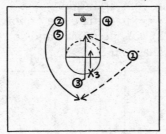

Diagram 8-14

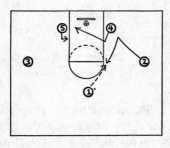

Diagram 8-15

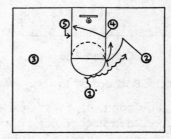

Diagram 8-16

POST UP OPTIONS FOR WING

These post up options are excellent for teams that possess a wing player with outstanding one-on-one ability, and also, if the personnel

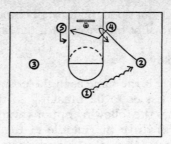

Diagram 8-17

of your team is made up of a point guard, two forwards for wings and two post men. If one of these forwards is consistently taller than the player defending him, a play must be provided to take advantage of the defender by posting him up inside.

There are three ways to initiate the options: (1) post option to wing (Diagram 8-15); (2) wing point pick-and-roll (Diagram 8-16); and (3) wing post up low (Diagram 8-17).

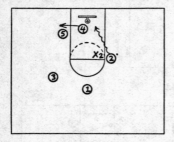

Diagram 8-18

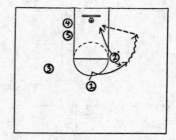

Diagram 8-19

Option 1: Post option to wing

The point, 01, calls "clear 04." Post, 04, moves halfway up the lane, and then stacks behind post, 05. At the same time, wing, 02, cuts on a backdoor-like cut, plants his right foot near the block, pivots, and cuts to the side high post to receive a pass from 01. If, upon receiving the ball, 02's defensive man has taken himself out of position by attempting to deny the pass, 02 makes a move down the lane for a shot (Diagram 8-18).

Diagram 8-19 illustrates the point, 01, breaking off the wing, 02, for a return pass. 01 has the option of taking a lay-up if he has his man beat, a jump shot after receiving the return pass from 01, or pass to 02 rolling down the lane if a switch occurs.

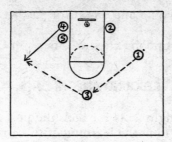

Diagram 8-20

If none of these options are available, 01 or 02 must look to turn the ball over to attack the weak side. 01 passes to the weakside wing, 03, at the top of key. If 03 is open, he takes a jump shot. If 03 is overplayed, he immediately breaks backdoor to the basket and stacks behind 05. At the same time, 04 moves from behind the stack to the top of the key for offensive balance and for a pass from 01.

In Diagram 8-20, upon receiving the ball, 03 passes to 04 breaking to the wing area from behind the stack. 04 has the following options available to him: (1) shoot a jump shot; (2) drive the middle of the lane for a lay-up or jump shot; (3) drive the baseline and shoot a jump shot; (4) pass to 05 posting up low; or (5) 05 can come out to screen 04 for a pick-and-roll.

These options have been previously described in Diagrams 8-10 and 8-11. After 03 passes to 04, he screens 01, so if 04 needs to continue the offense, 01 can continue it.

Option 2: Wing-point pick-and-roll

The wing-point pick-and-roll begins the same way as described in Option 1, with the only difference being, 02 screens 01. 02 sets a screen. 01 drives his defensive man into 02's screen and passes to 02 rolling down the lane. 04 stacks behind 05 and 03 moves to point area. 01 can shoot a jumper if his defensive man goes behind the screen.

The rest of the options are the same as described in Option 1.

Option 3: Wing post up low

Diagram 8-17 illustrates what happens when 01 calls "clear 04," and dribbles to the wing area. This keys wing, 02, to cut to the middle of the lane and cut back to the block to post up low. If 01 passes to 02,

02 has the option of going one-on-one or passing to 01 making a solo cut for a jump shot.

The remaining options are the same as in Option 1.

REBOUND ASSIGNMENTS

Rebounding assignments for both the post and clear series are the same, thus facilitating the learning of these responsibilities.

On the backdoor option to the wing in the post series, the rebound assignments are: 02, after the shot, fills ballside position, 05 fills the weakside position, 04 fills the middle position, 03 moves to the high rebound area, and 01 is the defensive safety.

The assignments on a shot by 01 breaking off the post (Diagram 8-2), or pick by 04 (Diagram 8-11) are: 01 fills ballside position, 02 fills weakside position, 05 fills the middle position, 04 fills high rebound area, and 03 becomes the defensive safety. When 04 goes one-on-one in the post series the rebound assignments are: 04 follows his shot and fills ballside low, 05 fills the middle position, 02 fills weakside low, 03 moves to the high rebound area, and 01 is the defensive safety.

On a shot by the low post, as shown in Option 4 of the post series (Diagram 8-7), and Option 2 of the clear series (Diagram 8-12) the assignments are: 04 fills ballside low post, 05 fills middle position, 02 fills low-post weak side, 01 moves to the high rebound area, and 03 is the defensive safety.

The rebound coverages on a shot by the weakside wing from the top of the key are: 04 fills low-post ballside, 02 fills low-post weak side, 05 fills the middle position, 03 covers high rebound area, and 01 becomes the defensive safety.

On a shot by 02 from the weakside options of the post and clear series the assignments are: 05 fills low-post ballside, 04 fills low-post weak side, 01 moves to cover the middle rebound position, 02 covers the high rebound area, and 03 is the defensive safety. The rebound responsibilities are the same if 02 drives baseline or middle.

POST AND CLEAR SERIES FROM SIX OTHER FORMATIONS

From a 1-3-1 alignment (Diagram 1-2), the post and clear series can be initiated in one of three ways, depending on the movements of the post men. The simplest method is for post 04 to remain stationary

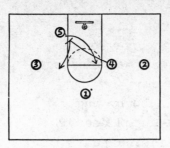

Diagram 8-21

at high side post, and post 05 to break to the opposite high side post. This movement creates a possible backdoor situation for wing, 03. The second method is a high-low screen illustrated in Diagram 8-21. This is the best method of getting into the post series. Post 04, breaks down on post 05, and then breaks to the side post. 05 breaks off the screen to where 04 vacated. The third method is for post 04, to slide across the lane to 05's side and for 05 to break to where 04 vacated.

From the 1-4 alignment (Diagram 1-3), the most important factor is how the post men break to the high-post area. The three methods are: break from the low post (Diagram 4-7), low-post interchange (Diagram 4-8), and x move (Diagram 4-9). From here on, you should now understand how the offense is initiated.

From the 1-4 low alignment (Diagram 1-4), the wings can clear quicker; the clear series is utilized from this set. The pick-and-roll between the point and post becomes a very strong two-man situation.

The stack alignments (Diagrams 1-5 and 1-6) use the same methods of initiating the offense as previously mentioned in the 1-3-1 and the 1-4 alignments.

To initiate the offense from the unbalanced stack (Diagram 1-7), the two post movements illustrated in Diagrams 4-12 and 4-13 are used.

As you can see, giving the post men the option of changing alignments creates multiple looks for the defense, even though the same offense is being utilized.

Here is a brief summary of the options of the post and clear series:

1. Post series

    a. Backdoor for onside wing

    b. Point breaking off post

      c. Post goes one-on-one

      d. Onside pivot posts low

      e. Jump shot by weakside wing

      f. Weakside play

          1) Jump shot by wing

          2) Post-wing pick-and-roll

          3) Wing pass to post

  2. Clear series

      a. Pick-and-roll

      b. Onside pivot posts up low

      c. Jump shot by weakside wing

      d. Weakside play

          1) Jump shot by wing

          2) Post-wing pick-and-roll

          3) Wing pass to post

9

Attacking
EVEN FRONT ZONE
Defenses

During the season, a team can expect to play against many different types of zone defenses. It is impossible for you, as a coach, to expect your players to learn a different offense for each zone defense that your team may face.

The Double Post Zone Offense has the same basic offensive principles as the man-to-man attack: (1) organized movement of the ball; (2) organized movement of players; (3) floor balance; (4) high percentage shots. The zone pattern, Blitz and Rotate, is basically the same pattern used against man-to-man. Tested over the years, the zone offense has been used successfully against a variety of zone defenses.

The next two chapters deal with a description of the modern zone defenses, plus shifts and slides. Each defense will be dealt with separately, illustrating its strengths and weaknesses, and how the Double Post Offense attacks each. The Double Post Zone Offense:

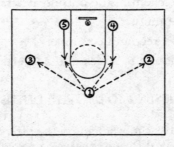

Diagram 9-1

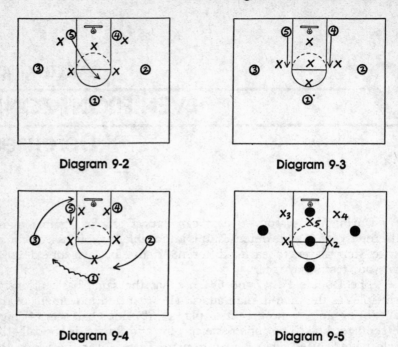

Diagram 9-2   Diagram 9-3

Diagram 9-4   Diagram 9-5

1. Provides at least four entry pass possibilities to initiate the offense (Diagram 9-1).

2. Creates a strong high- and low-post attack.

3. Establishes triangles and uses overload situations.

4. Provides opportunities for good shooters from 15- to 17-foot range.

5. Combines excellent inside-outside attack.

6. Provides continuity.

7. Provides good rebound coverage.

8. Is flexible enough to attack odd and even front defenses.

ADJUSTING TO DIFFERENT DEFENSES

The initial and basic movements of the offense are taught from a 1-2-2 alignment. It is best for the players to begin from positions with which they are familiar. After recognizing the defense, they can adjust quickly to the type of attack to be run against it. To see how to move to a 1-3-1, 1-4, or stack alignment to attack different zone defenses, see Diagrams 9-2 through 9-4, which illustrate these movements.

The 2-3 zone and 2-1-2 zone are the two major zones that use even fronts. The zones are very similar, but they differ with respect to how the defensive position of the post is played and how the offensive wings are covered.

ATTACKING A 2-3 ZONE

The 2-3 zone defense is the strongest defense under the basket, because there are more defensive players near the basket. The defense is used against teams that have strong, talented, big players or against teams that have weak-shooting perimeter players. It practically eliminates offensive rebounding formation. This defense's objective is to eliminate second shots and score by using the fast break.

Advantages

1. Provides good coverage against low-post play.
2. A natural rebound triangle is formed, which makes this a strong rebounding defense.
3. It is effective against a team that has weak outside shooters.
4. Converts well to fast break.

Weaknesses

1. Vulnerable against a good jump shot team from a 12- to 15-foot range on either side of free throw lane.
2. Weak against a high-post player who forces defensive post to come out to cover him (Diagram 9-5).
3. The gaps or seams between the two front players and three back players create problems concerning who has responsibility to cover these areas.

The basic shifts and slides of the players in the 2-3 zone are described below.

Guard responsibility

1. Both guards are responsible for keeping ball out of the high-post area.

2. Ballside guard, X1, has wing coverage.

3. Weakside guard, X2, has high-post coverage.

4. When ball is reversed, X2 checks point and moves to ballside coverage of 02. X1 moves across lane to cover high post.

Forward responsibility

1. When ball is passed to wing area, X4 must check quick shot opportunity until X2 can cover 02. X4 then moves to a position 6-8 feet outside of lane to help cover low-post area.

2. If ball is passed to corner, X4 moves out to cover 05. X3 helps on the weak side.

3. On a quick reverse, X3 must check quick shot opportunity until X1 can cover and defend low-post area.

Center responsibility

1. X5 must keep the ball from entering the low-post area.

2. X5 never moves more than halfway up the lane to cover high post. This is the guards' responsibility.

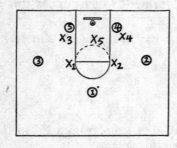

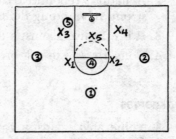

Diagram 9-6   Diagram 9-7

Zone Attack

The first area of concern against a 2-3 zone defense is the alignment that would place your players in the gaps or seams of the defense. This sets up shots from weak areas of the zone without movement. Also, it forces defensive adjustment because the defense is not in a natural match-up situation. Against a 2-3 zone, use one of three alignments (1-2-2, 1-3-1, or 1-4) to place your players in the gaps or seams as shown in Diagrams 9-6 through 9-8.

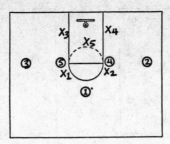

Diagram 9-8

After the alignment is chosen, you should be concerned with continually forcing the defense to make adjustments until you get the shot you want. Certain options within the offense will prove to be more effective.

An important area to follow in attacking a 2-3 zone is to overload the defense in its weak areas by using three perimeter players (point and two wings). The two defensive guards are forced to cover three offensive players. If they extend themselves from their normal defensive areas, this opens up the inside offense (high-low).

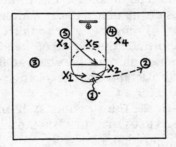

Diagram 9-9

Blitz and Rotate—Normal

The point guard, 01, must dribble in the gap between the two defensive guards and pass to the wing where pressure is greatest, as shown in Diagram 9-9. He should not pick up his dribble at the top of the key and let the defense cover the passing lanes.

In executing the play, the wing, 02, has four options: (1) he can shoot, (2) pass to 04, (3) pass to 05, and (4) dribble to the baseline.

In the first option (Diagram 9-9), 01 passes the ball to 02, 02

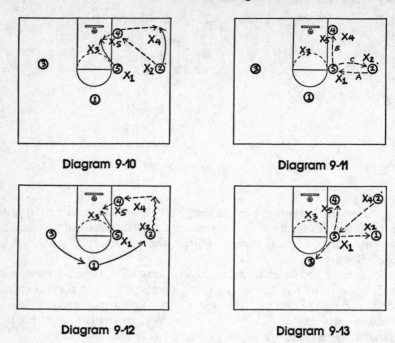

Diagram 9-10

Diagram 9-11

Diagram 9-12

Diagram 9-13

shoots. 05 sinks to and rebounds weak side (he must anticipate a shot). 04 rebounds strong side. 03 moves to the middle of lane to complete the rebound triangle. 01 remains at the top of key.

Diagram 9-10 illustrates the second option, 02 passing to 04 who can either make a power move or pass back to 02 who moves to the corner, in the event the defense should collapse, or, 04 can pass to 05 coming down the lane for a shot.

In Diagram 9-11, the third option is: 02 passes to 05 who can shoot a jump shot, pass to 04, pass to 03 on the weak side, or pass back out to 02 at the wing position.

The last option available to 02 is to dribble to the corner as illustrated in Diagram 9-12. 02's dribble forces X4 to cover him. If 02 cannot drive or shoot, he has the following options; (1) pass to 04 who can make a power move or pass to 05; (2) pass to 05 who can shoot a jump shot or pass to 04 (Diagram 9-13), pass to 03, or pass to 01; (3) 02 can pass the ball to 01 and cut through to the opposite wing. 01 then has all the options when the ball is at the wing position. (Diagram 9-10).

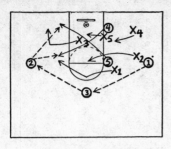

Diagram 9-14

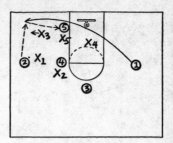

Diagram 9-15

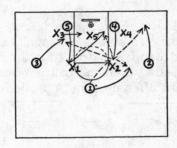

Diagram 9-16

If none of these options are available, 01 passes to 03, who in turn passes to 02. The post players cross with the high post breaking first and going low and the low post going high (Diagram 9-14). This puts pressure on the defensive pivot to cover 05, and X2 must move across the lane to cover 04 in the high post. 02 can pass to 05 or 04 (Diagram 9-14). 04 and 05 can pass to each other as previously mentioned.

Diagram 9-15 illustrates an option available to 01 when the ball is reversed. 01 can move to the corner on ballside. If done quickly, 02 can pass to 01 in the corner before X3 can cover, because X3's first responsibility is to check quick shot opportunities at the wing. 01 can shoot or pass to 05 on baseline side for a power move.

Initiate the blitz part of the offense with a pass to the post. 01 passes to 04. 04 immediately looks for 02 breaking to the corner, 05 breaking to the low post on ballside, or 03 breaking to the low post on the weak side as shown in Diagram 9-16. If the ball is passed to the wing area, the box is formed and the rotation part of the offense is in effect. 03 moves to the point.

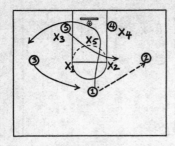

Diagram 9-17

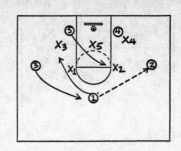

Diagram 9-18

Diagram 9-17 illustrates the weakside cut, and Diagram 9-18 shows the exchange between point and wing. These two moves serve the same purpose and are used to get a good shooting point guard to the wing position so that when the ball is reversed, a better shot opportunity exists. The offense is run as previously described.

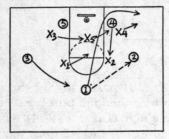

Diagram 9-19

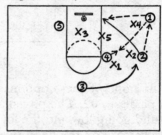

Diagram 9-20

Blitz and Rotate—Strongside Cut

The objective of the strongside cut is to overload one side of the court by sending the point guard to the corner. The wing, 02, upon receiving the ball from the point guard has three options: (1) he can shoot; (2) pass to 04; (3) pass to 01 in corner and cut.

In the first option (Diagram 9-19), 01 passes to 02 and cuts down the lane to the corner. If 02 shoots, 04 rebounds the strong side. 05 rebounds the weak side. 02 rebounds middle of lane after shot. 03 moves to top of key. 01 moves out to 02's wing position, If 02 cannot shoot, he looks to pass to 04, his second option.

The third option is for 02 to pass to 01 in the corner (Diagram 9-20). Here 02 passes to 01 in the corner; 02, the first cutter, breaks to

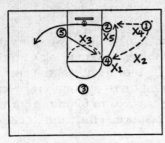

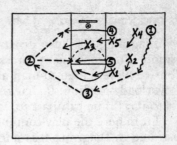

Diagram 9-21   Diagram 9-22

the basket. If 02 receives ball and shoots, 05 rebounds weak side, 04 has middle responsibility, and 03 protects defensively. X5 must prevent 02 from receiving the ball in the low-post area; 04 should be open if he has positioned himself between defender, X1, and the ball. 01 passes to 04 who can shoot or pass to 05 (Diagram 9-20). If 02 does not receive the ball, he continues to move across the lane to the wing position. 04 is the second cutter, breaking to the low-post area on ballside and looking for a pass from 01. 05 moves to high post also looking for a pass from 01 (Diagram 9-21). Both post men can utilize the high-low passes.

If 01 does not pass to either 04 or 05, 04 moves across lane to low-post area. 01 must dribble the ball out of the corner and pass to 03 (Diagram 9-22). 03 dribbles to the weak side and passes to 02 who has the following options: (1) he can shoot; (2) pass to 01, if 01 options to rotate to ballside corner (Diagram 9-15); (3) pass to 04 (Diagram 9-14); and (4) pass to 05 who has moved across lane to high post (Diagram 9-14).

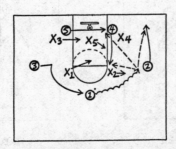

Diagram 9-23

Blitz and Rotate—Dribble Over

Diagram 9-23 illustrates the point man, 01, dribbling to the wing position. This movement forces the defensive players to pick up the offensive players man-to-man and with 05 moving across the lane to an overload situation. 01 has the following three options: (1) he can pass to 05; (2) he can pass to 04; (3) he can pass to 02 in the corner.

From here the play continues like the normal Blitz and Rotate as illustrated in Diagrams 9-11 and 9-12.

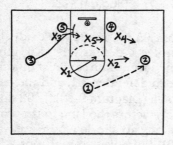

Diagram 9-24

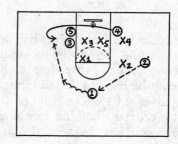

Diagram 9-25

Double Screen on Baseline

The play starts with a pass from 01 to 02, which shifts the defense, as shown as in Diagram 9-24. 03 moves to the low-post area to set a double screen with low post, 05. 02 passes back to 01, who in turn passes to 04 breaking under the double screen set by 03 and 05 (Diagram 9-25). If 04 cannot shoot, he passes back out to 01.

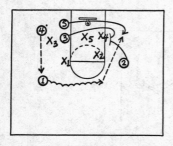

Diagram 9-26

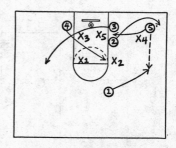

Diagram 9-27

Diagram 9-26 illustrates the continuation of the play with a double screen with 02. 04 passes to 01, while 03 moves across the lane to set a double screen with 02. 01 dribbles while 05 cuts under the double screen, then 01 passes to 05 for a short jump shot.

If a shot does not develop by this time, the players quickly move to form the box and enter into the Blitz and Rotate part of the offense, as illustrated in Diagram 9-27.

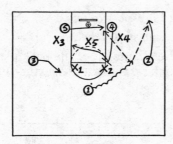

Diagram 9-28

Clear Series

In Diagram 9-28, 04 sets a screen on X2 (guard in a 2-3 zone), then rolls to the weakside low-post area; 05 moves across the lane behind X5, who has probably moved up several steps to check 04's movement; 02 slides to the corner; and 01 dribbles off of 04's screen for three options: (1) he can shoot; (2) he can pass to 05 moving to low post on ballside; and (3) he can pass to 02 in corner.

In the first option; 01 can shoot a jump shot if X4 does not come up to cover him. If 04 stops the jump shot, 01 passes to 02 who will be open in the corner for the second option. The third option is for 01 to pass to 05 on the low post. This option will be available if X5 has moved up the lane to check 04. The screening movement has created a 3-on-2 overload situation for X4 and X5 to cover, and a good shot should develop.

ATTACKING A 2-1-2 ZONE

The 2-1-2 zone is one of the most popular zone defenses. It

provides strong coverage under the basket and is used to stop a team with a strong high-post attack. The 2-1-2 zone, like the 2-3 zone, provides strong defensive rebounding. The defense can also move to fast break very well.

Advantages

1. It is effective against teams that do not possess strong outside shooters.
2. It is a strong high-post defense.
3. The defense is easy to teach.
4. Because of the alignment of the back players in the zone, the guards can pick up the offense further up the court than in a 2-3 zone.

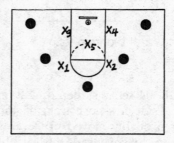

Diagram 9-29

Weaknesses

1. It is vulnerable against good shooters from the corner (Diagram 9-29).
2. The defensive pivot must move to cover low-post area, leaving the high-post area open to weakside cutters.
3. It is vulnerable against a team that shoots well from the outside wing area (Diagram 9-29).

The basic shifts and slides of the players in the 2-1-2 zone are:

Guard responsibility

1. Both guards play one step above the edge of the free throw circle, which is higher than in the 2-3 zone.

2. Ballside guard, X1, has wing coverage.

3. Weakside guard, X2, has high-post coverage.

4. When ball is reversed, X2 checks ball and moves to ballside coverage of 02. X1 moves across lane to cover high post.

Forward responsibility

1. X3 and X4's primary responsibility is to rebound.

2. If ball is passed to the wing position and the wing is deeper than foul line, X4 must come up to cover him.

3. When ball is passed to corner, X4 must move to cover the corner.

Center responsibility

1. When the ball is at the wing, X5 moves down the lane and plays above low post while X4 is in front.

2. If the ball is passed to the corner, X5 will have to move to cover the low post.

Zone Attack

With the exception of the high-post coverage and coverage of the corners, the 2-3 and 2-1-2 zone defenses are very similar. The alignments used to attack a 2-3 zone are the same ones used to attack a 2-1-2 zone (Diagrams 9-6 through 9-8). Probably the 1-2-2 alignment would be more effective against the 2-1-2 zone because the defensive post man is guarding empty space. The only adjustment to the alignments, whether it be 1-2-2, 1-3-1, or 1-4, would be to move the wings two feet below the foul line in the gaps of the defense. This would force the defensive forwards to come up to stop the jump shot, also leaving a temporary passing lane to the low-post area.

Our attack against a 2-1-2 zone is basically the same, except we run patterns that move the defensive forwards to cover the corners and force the defensive pivot to cover the low post, leaving the high-post area vacant.

Without the aid of diagraming, which would be repetitious, try to review and visualize the moves of the normal Blitz and Rotate attack with an emphasis on wing dribble to the corner (Diagrams 9-12 through 9-15); strongside cut, which is probably the best means of attack (Diagrams 9-19 through 9-22); dribble over (Diagram 9-23); double screen on baseline (Diagrams 9-24 through 9-27); and clear series (Diagram 9-28).

This concludes the discussion of the attack against even zone defenses. The next chapter covers the attack against odd front defenses.

10

Attacking
ODD FRONT ZONE
Defenses

There are three major types of zones using an odd front 1-2-2, 3-2, and 1-3-1. The strengths and weaknesses of each zone, and how each zone is attacked are presented in this chapter.

ATTACKING A 1-2-2 ZONE

The 1-2-2 zone is tough on the ball on the perimeter. This defense requires two strong, big men to play the back line. A good point guard is also required, since this defense converts to the fast break quicker than any other zone defense and is often used by teams that are geared to fast break.

Advantages

1. The defense is used by strong offensive teams.
2. Takes advantage of two tall players on a team.
3. Can easily form a rebound triangle.
4. Puts pressure on perimeter passing and shooting.
5. Good defense to trap from.

Weaknesses

1. Weak against an expert passing team.
2. Easy for offensive team to outnumber back two defenders (Diagram 10-1).
3. An area of the baseline can be easily overloaded.

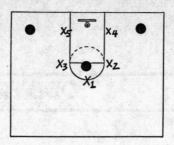

Diagram 10-1

4. The defense is weak to cover the corner.

5. Weak at high post (Diagram 10-1).

The basic shifts and slides of the players in the 1-2-2 zone are:

Point responsibility

1. Prevent good shots from point area.

2. Prevent passes to the high post.

3. Has high-post coverage when ball is at wing.

4. When ball is reversed, X1 checks ball and moves to high-post coverage when 01 passes to 03.

Wing responsibility

1. Wings, X2 and X3, must keep one foot in lane to prevent ball from entering high-post area from point.

2. X2 must pressure wing and take away his shooting opportunities when ball is passed from point to wing.

3. Weakside wing, X3, must be in a position to help on post coverage and rebounding.

4. When ball is passed to corner, he steps in the passing lane between wing and baseline player. If the offense has a strong post player, X2 would sag toward that player to prevent a pass. X3 moves to a position that is straight with the ball in corner.

5. Occasionally, X2 will be involved in a trap with one of the back men.

Post responsibility

1. X4 must front in low-post area; X5 must help out.

2. When ball is in corner, X4 must cover the corner hard to prevent shot. X5 must cover low post on ballside.

3. If there are offensive players in both high and low post, X4 covers high post and X5 covers low post.

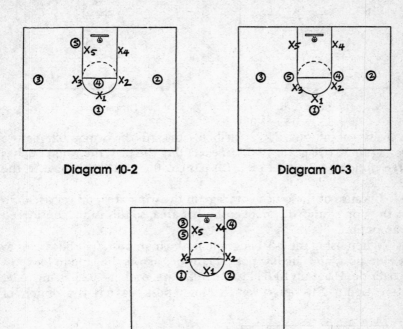

Diagram 10-2   Diagram 10-3

Diagram 10-4

Zone Attack

The alignments used to place players in the gaps of the defense would be 1-3-1, 1-4, and stack as illustrated in Diagrams 10-2 through 10-4. The attack against the 1-2-2 zone defense is aimed at the low-post, corner and high-post areas. It takes exceptional athletes to cover the back areas of the zone.

Blitz and Rotate—Normal

The point guard must be very concerned about getting the ball to the wing or the whole offense could go down the drain. A 1-3-1 alignment forces the defensive wings to prevent the ball from being passed to the high-post area, thus creating a better passing lane to the wing. If the point has problems passing to the wings, he dribbles toward the defensive wing to freeze him before passing the ball.

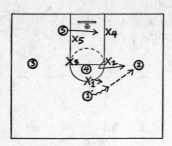

Diagram 10-5

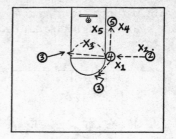

Diagram 10-6

The point guard, 01, dribbles toward the wing, 02, before passing to 02 (Diagram 10-5). In executing the play, the wing, 02, has three options: (1) pass to 04, (2) pass to 05, and (3) dribble to the baseline.

Because of the quick coverage in the wing area, 02 very seldom has the opportunity to shoot from that area, so this is not considered as an option.

When using the 1-3-1 alignment, the high post, 04, slides over to the side post, and the low post, 05, moves across the lane to low post on ballside. Diagram 10-6 illustrates 02's first option—02 passing to 04 before point, X1, can cover the high post. 04 has the option of

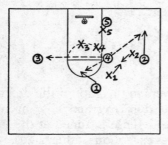

Diagram 10-7

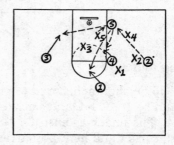

Diagram 10-8

shooting a jump shot, driving to the basket, passing to 05 at low post, passing to 03 on the weak side, or passing to 01 at the point. The defense must not let the ball get in high post without making an adjustment. Usually the defense will adjust by letting one of their post men cover the high post (Diagram 10-7). Since most defenses converge on the ball, X4, X2, and X1 surround 04. If 04 does not panic, he still can pass to 02 moving to the corner, 03 on the weak side, or 01 at the point.

In Diagram 10-8, 02 passes to 05. If the pass to 05 is complete, it is because X4 is sleeping or is outpositioned. If 05 receives ball, he can make a power move to the basket, pass to 04 moving down the lane, pass to 03 on weak side, or pass to 01 at the point.

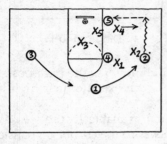

Diagram 10-9   Diagram 10-10

The third option is illustrated in Diagram 10-9 with 02 dribbling to the baseline. X4 must move to cover 02 in the corner for a jump shot. If X5 does not move quickly enough to cover 05 at low post, 02 can pass to 05. 05 then will have the same options as if 02 passed him the ball from wing.

If 02 cannot shoot or pass to 05, he looks to 01, who has moved to wing position. Once 02 passes the ball to 01, he moves to the weakside wing position (Diagram 10-10). If these options are not available, 01 passes the ball to 03, who in turn passes to 02 at the wing position. The high post, 04, breaks first going low, and the low post, 05, breaks to the high post (Diagram 10-11). X5 must defend the low-post area, and

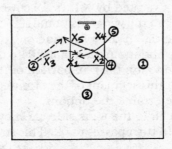

Diagram 10-11

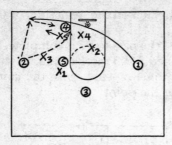

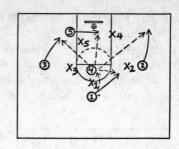

Diagram 10-12   Diagram 10-13

X1 must move to check 03 at point and defend 05 at the high post. 02 can pass to 04 low, or 05 high. 04 and 05 can execute their high-low passes as previously mentioned.

Diagram 10-12 illustrates the option available to the weakside wing, 01, when the ball is reversed. 01 moves to the corner on ballside. If X5 remains tight to cover 04, 02 can pass to 01 for a shot. If X5 moves to the corner to cover 01, 02 can pass to 04. 01 also can pass to 04 on baseline side for a power move.

The blitz part of the offense can be initiated (Diagram 10-13) from a 1-3-1 alignment. 01 passes to 04. 04 has the following options: (1) 04 can shoot or drive, (2) 04 can pass to 05, (3) 04 can pass to 02, (4) 04 can pass to 01, or (5) 04 can pass to 03.

This pass to 04 attacks the 1-2-2 zone at its weakest point. Once 04 has received the ball, the defense must make adjustments. These adjustments cause weaknesses elsewhere in the defense.

In Diagram 10-13, 01 has passed to 04. 04 immediately turns, faces the basket, and looks for a shot for the first option. If X4 moves out to defend 04, 04 passes to 02 moving toward baseline or passes to 05 moving to the area vacated by X4. If X2 covers 02 going baseline, 04 passes to 01 cutting to the wing position. If X5 moved across lane to cover 05, 04 passes to 03 on the weak side.

If none of these options are available, 04 passes to 01 or 03, who in turn passes to 01 to set up the box portion of the offense (Diagram 10-14). The options of this segment of the offense have been discussed enough for you to determine the options.

To reverse the ball to the weak side, 02 moves to the wing area, 01 passes to 03, who in turn passes to 02. This starts the rotation part of the offense.

You should be able to visualize the weakside cut and exchange between 01 and 03 against the 1-2-2 zone.

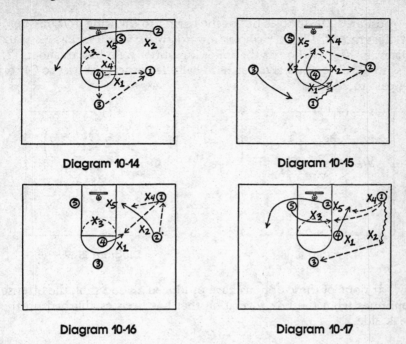

Diagram 10-14   Diagram 10-15

Diagram 10-16   Diagram 10-17

Blitz and Rotate—Strongside Cut

The strongside cut is a strong move against a 1-2-2 zone because it forces the defensive post man to cover the corner. The wing, 02, upon receiving the ball has three options: (1) pass to 01 cutting, (2) pass to 04, (3) pass to 01 in corner and cut.

In Diagram 10-15, 01 passes to 02 and cuts down the middle of the lane. Occasionally, X4 will not honor this cut and 02 will pass to 01 for a shot.

If 02 cannot pass to 01 for a shot or shoot himself, he passes to 04, his second option. The third option is for 02 to pass to 01 in the corner (Diagram 10-16). Here, 02 is the first cutter and breaks to the basket. 01 can pass to 02 or 04. 04 has a good chance of being open because 02's cut temporarily screens X5 from defending 04. If 02 does not receive ball, he continues to move across the lane to the wing position. 04 becomes the second cutter cutting to the low-post area on ballside looking for a pass from 01 (Diagram 10-17). 05 moves high post looking for a pass from 01. Both post men can utilize the high-low passes as previously mentioned.

If 01 does not pass to 04 or 05, 04 moves across the lane to the low-post area. 01 dribbles out of the corner to the wing and passes to 03 (Diagram 10-17). 03 dribbles towards weak side and passes to 02 (Diagram 10-18), who has the following options: (1) he can shoot; (2) pass to 01, if he options to rotate to ballside corner; (3) pass to 04; or (4) pass to 05.

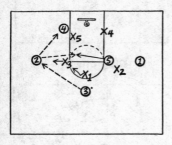

Diagram 10-18

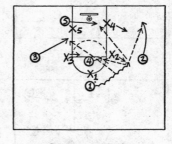

Diagram 10-19

If none of these options have produced a good shot, the offense continues from the box formation that has been established on the weak side.

Blitz and Rotate—Dribble Over

In Diagram 10-19, 01 dribbles the ball over to the right wing. X1 and X2 cover 01's movement. 02 moves baseline. 04 moves to side high post. 05 moves across the lane to an overload situation. 01 has four options: (1) pass to 02, (2) pass to 04, (3) pass to 05, and (4) pass to 03. From here the play continues like the normal Blitz and Rotate.

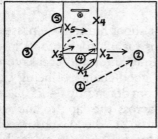

Diagram 10-20

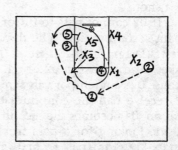

Diagram 10-21

Double Screen on Baseline

The play starts with a pass from 01 to 02. The defense must shift to honor this pass. 03 moves to the low post to set a double screen with 05 on X5 (Diagram 10-20). This should be easier to execute against two post defenders than against the three defenders in the 2-3 zone. 02 passes back to 01, who must dribble towards the weak side to force X3 to commit. 04 cuts behind the double screen and receives a pass from 01 (Diagram 10-21). If 04 cannot shoot, he passes back out to 01.

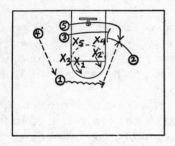
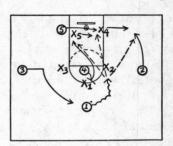

Diagram 10-22   Diagram 10-23

Diagram 10-22 illustrates the continuation of the play with a double screen on the other side of the lane set by 02 and 03. 01 dribbles across the top of the key while 05 cuts under the double screen, then 01 passes to 05 for the shot.

If a shot does not develop, the players move to form the box on the ballside and enter into the Blitz and Rotate part of the offense.

Clear Series

The Clear series is extremely successful against a 1-2-2 zone because it overloads the baseline area, and there are not enough men to cover the available options. In Diagram 10-23, 01 dribbles off the screen set by 04 on X1. 04 rolls to the weakside low-post area. 05 moves to ballside low post and 02 moves to the baseline. 03 moves to the top of key. 01 has the following options: (1) pass to 02, (2) pass to 05, (3) pass to 04, and (4) pass to 03.

In the first option, X4 must make a decision on covering 02 in the corner. If X4 stays home, 01 passes to 02 for a shot, or passes to 05. If X4 goes to the corner to cover 02, 01 passes to 05 for the second option. If X5 moves across the lane to cover 05, 01 can pass to 04 located at the weakside post. If none of the above options produce a good shot, 01 passes back out to 03 and the rotation part of the offense continues.

Single Screen on Post

Occasionally, we use the stack alignment with a two-guard front against a 1-2-2 zone. 02 dribbles to the gap of X1 and X2. 03 moves from the stack to the corner on ballside. 04 screens X5 and 05 cuts over the screen to low-post area. 02 can pass to 05 or 03, who in turn can pass to 05 (Diagram 10-24).

If a shot does not develop, 02 moves out to the wing position. 03 passes to 02, who dribbles into the gap of X1 and X2 before passing to 01. 03 moves across the baseline (Diagram 10-25). 01 has the following options: (Diagrams 10-26); (1) he can shoot, (2) he can pass to 03, and (3) he can pass to 05.

The screening technique by 04 creates defensive problems for the post men, X4 and X5, in covering 03 in the corner and 05 in the low post. The screening action continues until a good shot develops.

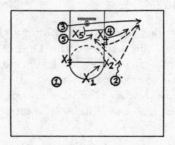

Diagram 10-24

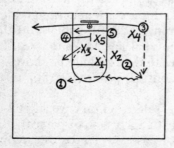

Diagram 10-25

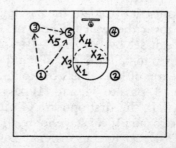

Diagram 10-26

ATTACKING A 3-2 ZONE

The 3-2 is a very popular zone defense. It is a good defense for a tall team that does not possess good speed. A team with a tall point guard that is agile is also an advantage for this defense. Like the 1-2-2 zone, this defense converts to the fast break quickly. The idea behind the defense is to shut off the inside play and force the ball around the perimeter. The defense defends the high-post area better than in the 1-2-2.

Advantages

1. The defense is passive, encouraging the offense to commit itself first.
2. By laying back or sagging, it forces the outside shot.
3. Players are in good position to fast break.
4. Protects the high-post area.

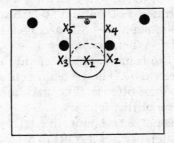

Diagram 10-27

Weaknesses

1. Easy for the offensive team to outnumber back defenders (Diagram 10-27).
2. Seam between front line and back two defenders is weak.
3. Offense can be overloaded.
4. Rebounding coverage is a problem, since the rebound triangle develops naturally.
5. Weak in covering corner.

The shifts and slides of the players in a 3-2 zone are:

Point responsibility

1. Prevent passes to the high-post area from front and wing area.
2. A variation of the 3-2 zone is for the point to slide down the lane, giving the defense a 2-1-2 look. This is a strong option for the defense if they possess a tall point guard.

Wing responsibility

1. Wings, X3 and X4, play wider than in the 1-2-2, because they do not have high-post responsibility.
2. Otherwise, review wing responsibility in 1-2-2 zone. They are the same.

Post responsibility

1. Post responsibility is the same as played in 1-2-2.

Zone Attack

The double post alignments used to attack a 3-2 zone defense are the same as the ones used to attack a 1-2-2 zone, which are 1-3-1, 1-4, or stack as illustrated in Diagrams 10-2 through 10-4.

With the exception of high-post coverage, the 1-2-2 zone and 3-2 zone are very similar. When using the 1-3-1 alignment, the point guard must force X1 to come out and defend the key area. This will open up a passing area to 04. The 1-4 alignment provides us with easy first-pass entries into the offense. The stack alignment immediately overloads the backline of the defense.

The attack does not vary against the defense. The only possible problem against the defense is if it shifts to 2-1-2 zone when the ball is located at the wing. The players must be ready to adjust to the change by running a strong side cut to force X1 to be mismatched at low post.

ATTACKING A 1-3-1 ZONE

This defense is effective against teams that attack the high- and low-post areas and on the wings. The 1-3-1 defense is especially suited for stopping the big pivot man that is a dangerous scorer near the basket. The objective is to keep three men between the ball and the basket at all times. This defense can be played as a basket-type defense or as an aggressive trapping defense.

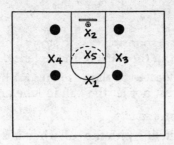

Diagram 10-28

Advantages

1. Covers the basic areas of attack—wing, high post, and low post.
2. Can adjust to a variety of offensive attacks.
3. Stops the good big man.
4. Good defense to stunt from.

Weaknesses

1. Corner areas are weak (Diagram 10-28).
2. Seams or gaps between point and wings provide opportunities for good shots.
3. This is a weak zone for rebounding.
4. This is a difficult zone to fast break from.

The basic shifts and slides of the players are:

Point responsibility

1. X1 can attack the ball at midcourt, halfway between the top of key and the midcourt area.
2. X3 prevents a direct pass from wing area. He forces guard to lob or bounce pass. X4, weakside wing, has one foot in the lane and has the responsibility of protecting basket area.
3. When ball is at the baseline, X3 plays in the passing lane between 04 and 02.

Post responsibility

1. His defensive responsibility is to stop all offensive penetration that comes from the gaps of the defense.
2. When ball is located at the baseline, X5 has low-post responsibility. He must not let the ball in lane area.

Baseline man's responsibility

1. X2 must stay in line with the ball when it is located in the front court and protect the low-post area at the same time.
2. When ball is located at deep baseline position, X2 must cover, not letting player drive baseline.
3. When the ball is reversed, X2 must move to the lane area in as straight line as possible, then proceed to baseline area on other side of court when ball is passed there.

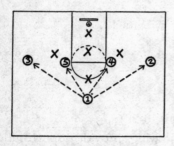

Diagram 10-29

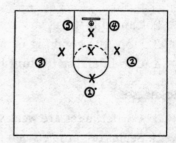

Diagram 10-30

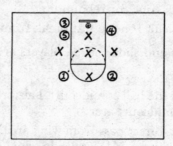

Diagram 10-31

Zone Attack

In attacking the 1-3-1 defense, we use either a 1-4, 1-2-2, or stack alignment, as shown in Diagrams 10-29 through 10-31. The attack against the defense is aimed at the gaps between point and wings, corners, and area left open when baseline man and post shift to cover corner and low post. The Blitz and Rotate is more effective from a 1-4 alignment.

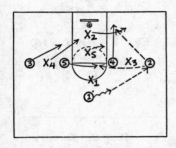

Diagram 10-32

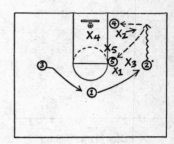

Diagram 10-33

Blitz and Rotate—Normal

In Diagram 10-32, 02 has little opportunity of shooting after receiving the ball from 01. 02 has three options: (1) pass to 04, (2) pass to 05, and (3) dribble to the baseline.

With 02's first option taken away from him by the defensive play of X2, 02 will pass to 04 sliding down the lane to the low-post area, or 02 will pass to 05 moving across the lane to the high post. Because of the natural matchup of the 1-3-1 against these offensive movements, it is very rare to get a shot from these movements.

When 02 dribbles to the baseline, this initiates his third option. It forces X2 to cover the corner, leaving 04 open for split second, and with X5 moving down the lane to cover the low post, 05 will be open at the high post (Diagram 10-33). 02 can pass to 04 or 05. The high-low passing between 04 and 05 is evident if the post men have positioned themselves properly. If neither man is open, 02 passes to 01, who has moved to the wing position. After 02 passes to 01, he moves to the weakside wing position (Diagram 10-34). If these options are not available, 01 passes to 03. As the defense shifts to expect the reversal of the ball, X1 moves to cover 03. 03 can pass to 05, who can shoot or pass to 04 at low post, as illustrated in Diagram 10-35. If 03 cannot pass to 05, he passes to 02 at the wing position. The high post, 05, breaks first going low, and low post, 04, breaks to the high post (Diagram 10-36). 02 can pass to 04 or 05.

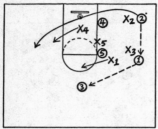

Diagram 10-34

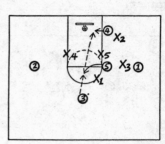

Diagram 10-35

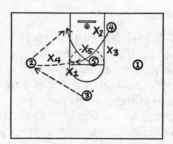

Diagram 10-36

If the weakside wing, 01, moves to the corner on ballside as shown in Diagram 10-37, 02 can pass to 01. X2 will move to cover 01 in the corner. X3 will move to cover low post. 01 can pass to 04 on baseline side for power move, or to 05, who can shoot or pass to 03 on the weak side.

The blitz part of the offense is very effective against the 1-3-1 zone from a 1-4 alignment. 01 passes to 04 (Diagram 10-38). 04 has the following options: (1) he can shoot, (2) pass to 02, (3) pass to 05, (4) pass to 01, and (5) pass to 03.

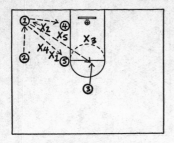

Diagram 10-37

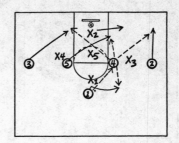

Diagram 10-38

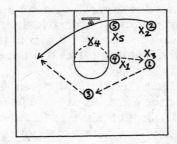

Diagram 10-39

The pass to 04 puts pressure on the defensive man, X2. With 02 and 05 both breaking to the same side, X2 must make a decision—either one provides an opening. 04 can pass to 05, who shoots. If 04 cannot pass to 05, he can pass to 02 in the corner. If neither 05 nor 02 are open, 04 can pass to 01 breaking to the wing vacated by 02, or pass to 03 on the weak side.

If none of these options are available, 04 passes to 01 or 03 to set up the box portion of the offense (Diagram 10-39). To reverse the ball to the weakside 02 moves to the wing area, 01 passes to 03, who in turn passes to 02. This starts the rotation part of the offense.

Blitz and Rotate—Strongside Cut

The strongside cut forces X2 to move to the corner to cover 01. Once the ball is passed to 02 (Diagram 10-40), 02 can pass to 01 or 04. If 02 passes to 04 at high post, 04 can shoot or pass to 05, who has moved to weakside low post. Diagram 10-41 shows the options

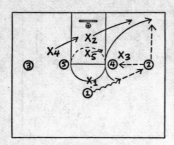

Diagram 10-40

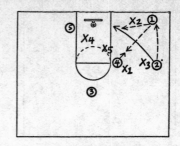

Diagram 10-41

available to 01. 01 can pass to 02 breaking toward the basket. The cut by 02 forces X5 to cover 02, leaving 04 open for a shot. If 02 does not receive the ball, he continues to move across the lane to the wing position. 04 breaks to the low post. 05 moves to the high post. Both post players can use the high-low passes that are effective against all zones.

If 01 cannot pass to either of the post men, 04 moves across the lane. 01 dribbles out to the wing and passes to 03 (Diagram 10-42). 03 dribbles towards weak side and passes to 02, who has the following options (Diagram 10-43): (1) he can shoot; (2) pass to 01, if he options to rotate to ballside corner; (3) pass to 04; and (4) pass to 05.

When 01 has the ball in the corner against a 1-3-1 zone defense, all the players must be aware of a possible trap. If the trap occurs before 02 cuts through, 01 should be able to pass to 04 low, 05 high, and 03 at the wing position. If 02 has already cut through, the players must react immediately or possibly lose the ball. 03 must move to the wing quickly to provide a release for 01 (Diagram 10-44).

From here the offense continues as has been illustrated throughout this chapter.

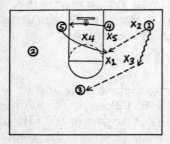

Diagram 10-42

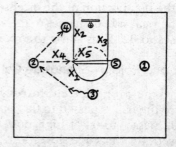

Diagram 10-43

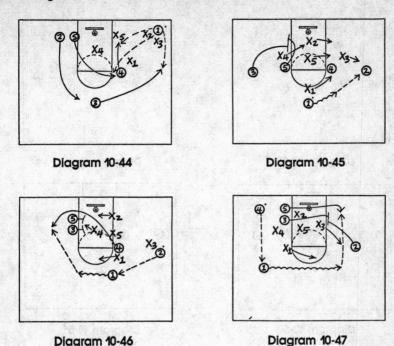

Diagram 10-44   Diagram 10-45

Diagram 10-46   Diagram 10-47

Double Screen on Baseline

The play starts with a pass from 01 to 02 to shift the defense. 05 slides down the lane on the weak side, while 03 moves to set a double screen with him as illustrated in Diagram 10-45. 02 passes to 01, who dribbles toward the weak side to force X3 to commit. 01 passes to 04 cutting behind the double screen (Diagram 10-46). If 04 cannot shoot, 04 passes to 01.

Diagram 10-47 illustrates the continuation of the play with a double screen on the other side of the lane by 02 and 03. 01 dribbles across the top of the key while 05 cuts under the double screen, then 01 passes to 05 for the shot. If a shot does not develop, the players move to form the box and enter into Blitz and Rotate part of the offense.

Single Screen on Post

The stack alignment with a two-guard front against a 1-3-1 zone is also used. The shift to a two-guard front has already been explained. 02 dribbles into the gap of X1 and X3. 03 moves to the

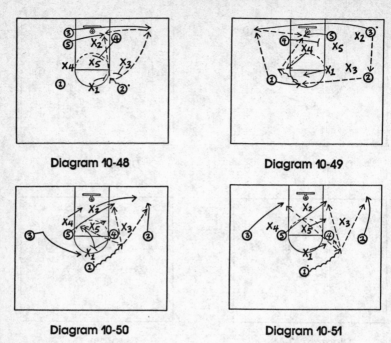

Diagram 10-48   Diagram 10-49

Diagram 10-50   Diagram 10-51

corner on ballside, forcing X2 to cover him. 04 screens X5 and 05 cuts under the screen for pass from 02 or 03, as illustrated in Diagram 10-48.

If a shot does not develop, 02 moves out to the wing position and dribbles into the gap of X1 and X2 before passing to 01. 03 moves to the opposite corner. 01 dribbles into the gap of X1 and X4. 04 screens X5 and 05 cuts under the screen for a pass from 01 or 03 (Diagram 10-49). The screening action on X5 continues until a good shot develops.

Clear Series

The clear series is extremely effective against the 1-3-1 zone, as it was against the 1-2-2 zone, because it overloads the baseline area. In Diagram 10-50, 04 screens X1 and rolls to the weakside post. 05 moves to ballside low post and 02 moves to the baseline. 03 moves to the top of the key. 01 has the following options: (1) pass to 02, (2) pass to 05, (3) pass to 04, and (4) pass to 03.

Remember that X5's major responsibility is to prevent penetration. 01's dribble over the screen keeps X5 near the foul line. X2 must make a choice between covering the low post or the corner. If none of the options produce a good shot, 01 passes back out to 03 and the rotation part of the offense continues.

Dribble Over

The four options of the dribble over force the baseline man, X4, to cover the corner. The options for 01 are: (1) pass to 04, (2) pass to 05, (3) pass to 02, and (4) pass to 03.

In Diagram 10-51, 01 dribbles over toward the wing position, 02 moves to the baseline, 05 cuts behind X5 to low post on the ballside, 03 breaks to weakside low post, and 04 remains at side high post. If X2 stays in the lane area, 01 passes to 02 in corner and X5 stays high to cover 04; 01 passes to 05 at low post. 01 can pass to 04, who can pass to 05 or 03, if X5 defends 05 at the low post. 01 can pass to 03 at the weakside post for a shot if X4 does not cover his area.

SUMMARY

Modern zone defenses are becoming increasingly complicated. It is not uncommon for the defense to show one alignment and then shift to another form or variation to confuse the offense.

The Double Post offense has shown different attacks against each of the traditional zone defenses with the same patterns, but has exploited the weaknesses of each defense with organized ball and player movements. The Double Post Offense offers:

1. At least four entry passes.
2. Strong high-low post attacks.
3. Overload situations.
4. Good shot opportunities from 15 feet.
5. Excellent post-perimeter attack.
6. Continuity.
7. Good rebound coverage.
8. Attacks against odd and even defenses.

Coaching the
DOUBLE POST
Fast Break

The fast break should be a definite part of your offensive philosophy. Your main objective is to get the ball up-court quickly and take a high percentage shot whenever possible. This is not to imply that you should run and gun, but you should use an organized method of bringing the ball up-court after a missed or made shot. Each player has responsibilities that require specific movement and precise timing.

Always break under control, and be ready to pull up if the opportunity for a high percentage shot is not there. If this happens, go into your secondary offense before you get into your regular offense.

Every coach must decide early in the season how fast and with what degree of freedom he going to allow his players to play. This must be based on the ball-handling ability of the players. Mistakes are going to be made, but the fewer turnovers, the more successful the fast break will be.

We fast break for the following reasons:

1. Fans love it.
2. It provides the highest percentage shots—lay-up and short jump shots.
3. It enables us to use more players, which helps make the whole team happy.
4. It gives the players freedom to use their individual abilities.
5. It helps condition our players.
6. It makes us more aggressive on defense.

The fast break can be broken down into five areas, which are essential for success. These areas are: (1) obtaining possession of the ball; (2) outlet; (3) distribution; (4) getting a high percentage shot; and (5) secondary offense.

OBTAINING POSSESSION OF THE BALL

Rebounding is the primary means of initiating the fast break. The average team misses 55 percent of its field goal attempts and 30 percent of foul shot attempts. To fast break consistently, you must control the boards, and a great deal of time must be spent on rebounding in pre-season and off-season.

The rebounding philosophy is simple. The players must assume that every shot will be missed and that they must gain possession of the ball. Stress forming a rebound triangle and assign rebounding responsibilities, regardless of where the shot is taken. All five players are to rebound, so it's important for perimeter and post players to know how to make front and reverse pivots.

On defense, box out all offensive players whether it be man or zone. The rule is to adjust to the man, not the ball. Boxing out tends to be more consistent. We want our rebounders to (1) get position, (2) box out, and (3) go to the ball.

Position

The most important skill that a rebounder has to develop is positioning, especially if he has to overcome lack of jumping ability or height. The position for rebounding begins when the defensive player first anticipates a shot. The rebounder must find his man or offensive player in his area and box him out. His body should be slightly bent with the knees flexed, hands held above head, arms and forearms spread to take up as much space as possible. The rebounder should make himself as big as possible.

Boxing Out

Two techniques used to develop boxing out position are the front pivot and reverse pivot. Most players want to go directly to the ball, instead of making contact with their opponent and then going to the ball, so the habit of pivoting must be practiced daily.

1. *Front pivot.* The front pivot is used when the offensive player is very close to the basket or one step away. Your player executes the pivot by stepping directly in front of the opponent and placing his foot outside of the offensive player's foot. Eye contact should be maintained during pivot to read the movement of the offensive player. After the pivot, contact should be felt on the buttock. The rebounder should have a comfortable, wide stance; weight on balls of feet; knees flexed; head up; arms extended shoulder level; and hands up, ready for the rebound.

2. *Reverse pivot.* The reverse pivot is used when the offensive player is farther from the basket, giving the rebounder more time to anticipate his cut. To execute the pivot, the rebounder moves laterally in the direction of the offensive player, pivots on the foot closest to the player, and swings his other foot around in front of the opponent. After the pivot, contact and position are the same as with a front pivot.

Going for the Ball

After positioning and boxing out, the rebounder must locate the basketball and then get it. A continual effort in practice must be made to prevent preoccupation with positioning and boxing out, and not getting the ball. In going after the ball the player should jump to his peak with arms extended and grasp the ball with a strong grip; upon gaining control of the ball, he should make a half turn in the air toward the side line, looking to the outlet areas to start the break. With constant practice, players will develop the ability to throw the outlet pass while in the air.

OUTLET PASS

After gaining possession, the rebounder should pivot to the outside, facing the sideline and pass to the outlet player with either a baseball pass or a two-handed overhead pass. The two-handed overhead pass is the safest. The ball should be cleared to the side between extended and hash mark, about three feet from sideline, away from traffic. This is the most important pass in the break because it puts the ball ahead of the defense. The primary responsibility of the rebounder is to start the break without throwing the ball away.

If a quick outlet pass cannot be made, the rebounder should start the break with a dribble, angling toward the sideline, keeping in mind that the outlet players should be open around midcourt after several dribbles. Outlet players should always be prepared to come back and help the rebounder in case he gets into trouble.

DRILLS TO DEVELOP REBOUNDING

In the rebounding drills, look for aggressive players. The drills in this chapter are concerned with pivoting, position, boxing out, gaining possession, and the outlet pass. The drills are presented in an order to help teach the techniques in a proper sequence.

Front and Reverse Pivot Drills

The players line up in three lines spread along the baseline, facing the coach at the top of the key. The first player in each line must use a front or reverse pivot to box out the offensive player. The coach designates the direction the offense is to move. Defense has their backs to the coach. Defenders must keep contact as long as possible. The offensive players go to the basketball, which is placed at the top of key. The players rotate to the back of each line until each player has had a turn or until the coach is satisfied with the performances of the players. Emphasis of this drill is on the pivoting and on maintaining contacts, which are so important in developing strong rebounders.

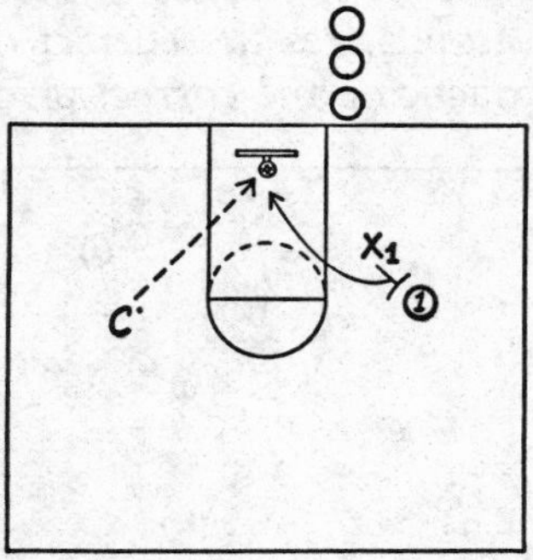

Diagram 11-1

One-on-One Rebounding

The one-on-one rebounding drill is practiced from the foul line and each wing (Diagram 11-1). Players form one line, with the first player acting as the rebounder. If the coach shoots, X1 boxes out 01 and rebounds the ball. The coach can pass the ball to 01, who shoots from a stationary or dribbling (allow one dribble) position. X1 boxes 01 out and goes to the basketball. The players rotate from offense to defense to end of line.

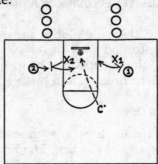

Diagram 11-2

Strongside-Weakside Rebounding

Position the players as illustrated in Diagram 11-2. Player X1 will execute a front pivot on 01 on the strong side of the court, and X2 will execute a reverse pivot on the weak side of the court when the coach shoots. The players rotate from offense to defense to the end of the other line. This drill emphasizes the correct distance from the ball used in our defense practicing the correct pivots.

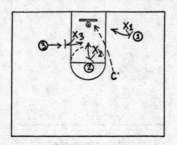

Diagram 11-3

Three-on-Three Rebounding Position Drill

Position the players as illustrated in Diagram 11-3. Players X1, X2, and X3 assume correct defensive positioning according to the location of the offensive players 01, 02, and 03, and the ball (Coach). The drill begins with the players in stationary positions with you (or the manager) shooting from different areas on the court. You can stop and correct the position of the rebounders if needed.As rebounding position improves, you (or manager) will pass to one of the offensive players. This pass keys offensive movement. The rebounders must adjust their positions according to their movement and rebound the ball when it is shot. When the ball is rebounded by a defensive player, he immediately makes the outlet pass to you (or manager). The players rotate from offense to defense to end of line.

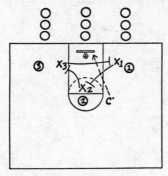

Diagram 11-4

Three-on-Three Rotation

The players position themselves as illustrated in Diagram 11-4. As the coach shoots, X1 boxes out 02, X2 boxes out 03, and X3 boxes out 01. Teach this drill first from a stationary position, then permit the offense to move. Players rotate from offense to defense to end of line.

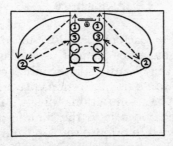

Diagram 11-5

Outlet Passing Drill

Position the players in two lines facing the backboard with one player in each of the outlet areas (Diagram 11-5). The first man in each line, 01, tosses the ball high on the backboard. He rebounds the ball, half turns to the side lines, and throws a two-handed overhead pass to the outlet receiver, who makes a two-handed chest pass to the next player in line, 03. The drill continues until each player has made an outlet pass twice, and each line changes sides.

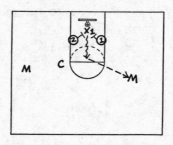

Diagram 11-6

Bust Out Drill

The players line up as shown in Diagram 11-6. You shoot and X1, the rebounder, grabs the ball off the backboard. Upon his landing on the floor 01 and 02 double team X1. The rebounder must protect the ball, leading with his head and shoulders and stepping between 01 and 02. Once through the defenders, he takes two dribbles and passes to one of the managers in the outlet area. Players then move to the end of line, and three more players take their place.

DISTRIBUTION

The easiest way to teach proper distribution of the break is from a 2-3 zone set. On any shot attempt each player must block out, regardless of where the offensive players are located in order to get the ball first. After you gain possession, players explode from the defensive board. All players must think "break." Make an outlet pass to the outside and then move it to the middle as soon as possible. Defense is now changed to offense with appropriate symbols.

When the middle player receives the ball, he maintains possession all the way to the foul line area before passing off for a score. If the ball cannot be taken down the middle, it is passed or dribbled down the side line.

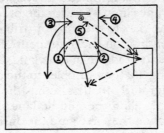

Diagram 11-7

The general plan of distribution, when the defensive rebound is secured by players 05 or 04, is to pass out to 02, who has moved to the outlet area side line extended as illustrated in Diagram 11-7. Occasionally, the outlet pass can be made to 01 in the middle. 01 sprints up the middle lane, anticipating a pass from 02. If 01 receives a pass from 02, he dribbles the ball down the middle lane. 02 fills right outside lane; 03 explodes down the left lane. 04 becomes the trailer and 05 the safety as shown in Diagram 11-8. It is important for 05 to stay 5 to 7 yards behind the play in case the ball is lost.

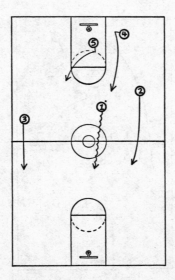

Diagram 11-8

On all situations the middle player on the break should be under complete control and thinking how to penetrate the defense and to which side of the court he should go with the pass. Upon reaching the defensive player, he can pass to the wing or dribble to the right or left of the foul lane, depending on the alignment of the defense.

If 02 cannot pass to 01 in the middle lane, 01 sprints up the side line that 02 is occupying. 02 then dribbles to the middle and advances the ball up-court (Diagram 11-9). 02 also has the option of passing to 01 on the side line and filling the middle lane (Diagram 11-10). The rebounder always becomes the safety and the onside forward (side ball was outletted) becomes the trailer.

If 04 secures the rebound and cannot pass directly to 02, he can dribble toward the side line, passing to 02 as soon as an opening develops. Diagram 11-11 shows the distribution of players.

If the ball is rebounded by 03, follow the same steps except have 04 fill the outside lane.

This is the simplest fast break distribution from a 2-3 set, however, these are the most likely to succeed and are easier for the player to understand.

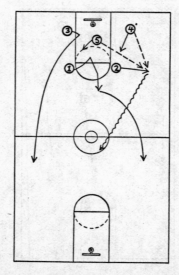

Diagram 11-9

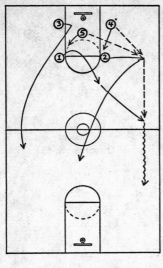

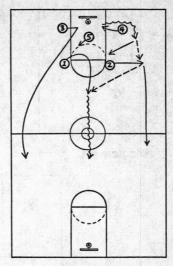

Diagram 11-10   Diagram 11-11

SITUATION: GETTING A HIGH PERCENTAGE SHOT

To be a successful fast break team, your players must look and take the best available shots possible on each break opportunity. Sometimes this might be a lay-up or a short jump shot. To help the players make the proper choice, practice four situations daily. This aids the players in understanding the correct play in each situation. The four situations are 2-on-1, 3-on-1, 3-on-2 versus tandem defense, and 3-on-2 versus split defense.

On all situations the middle player on the break should be under complete control and thinking how to penetrate the defense and to which side of the court to go with the pass. Upon reaching the defensive player, he can pass to the wing or dribble to the right or left of the foul lane depending on the alignment of the defense.

2-on-1

Players should be 12 to 15 feet apart. Pass back and forth to keep the defense from anticipating a move. But if you do not possess good ball handlers, the player with the ball should drive to the basket forcing the defender to pick him up and then pass off. Players must get the lay-up—no short jumpers—attempting to get the three-point play.

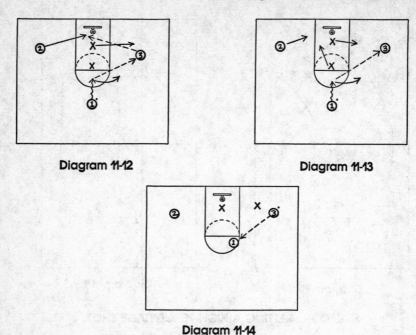

Diagram 11-12

Diagram 11-13

Diagram 11-14

3-on-1

Spread the players wide, keeping proper distribution. If wing players are ahead of the ball, they must not break to the basket until they reach the foul line extended. Then they should break to the basket at a 45-degree angle. The middle man stops at the foul line and takes one step to the side of his pass. Wing players that do not receive the ball must stop at the foul lane and fade to the corner. Players should be prepared to rebound a missed shot.

3-on-2 Versus Tandem Defense

The middle player, 01, dribbles to an area between the top of key and foul line and forces the defensive player to defend him. When 01 passes to 03 and back defender moves out to cover 03; 03 passes to 02 for a lay-up (Diagram 11-12). If the back defender in the tandem is slow in reacting to the pass to 03 from 01, and the front defender covers the basket area, 03 shoots the 15-foot shot (Diagram 11-13). If 03 and 02 are covered, 03 should look toward the foul lane area where 01 has stepped in the direction of the pass, looking for a return pass (Diagram 11-14).

3-on-2 Versus Split Defense

If the defense is split, the middle man, 01, should penetrate all the way to the basket if the defense allows. If his penetration is stopped, he passes to the open man from the side from which the pressure is applied.

SECONDARY OFFENSE

Some years you will have enough skilled players to handle 4-on-3 and 5-on-4 situations. The secondary offense is in between the fast break situations (2-on-1, 3-on-1, 3-on-2) and setting up against a 5-on-5 defense. There is a period of time the defense is not organized and you must try to take advantage of it.

4-on-3

This develops if, when advancing the ball up-court, the players recognize three defensive players. This is when the trailer becomes involved in the break. 01 dribbles to one side of the key area. 04 moves opposite of 01 to the side of the foul line for a possible pass from 01. If 04 is open, 01 passes to him for a short jump shot (Diagram 11-15). 01 also has the option to pass to 03, who in turn looks for 04 breaking to the block on ballside (Diagram 11-16).

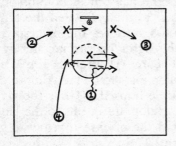   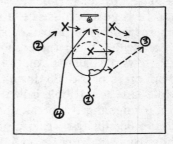

Diagram 11-15   Diagram 11-16

5-on-4

If a 4-on-3 situation does not produce a high percentage shot, the break is not over yet because a 5-on-4 situation might develop. With 03 having possession of the ball at wing area, 05, the safety, moves to the high side post away from the ball. 03 passes to 01, who in turn passes to 02 for a shot at the baseline (Diagram 11-17).

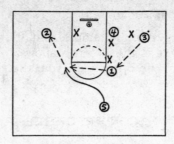

Diagram 11-17

If none of these options are available, 05 moves to low-post weak side to complete the offensive set. It is very important for 01 to pass to the wing to put pressure on the defense. Also, the movement of 05 and 04 going to the blocks forces the defense to cover the post area, thus producing medium range jump shots.

FAST BREAK FROM MADE FIELD GOAL

The second most frequent opportunity for a fast break occurs after a made field goal. For a brief instance after scoring, the defense relaxes and a quick throw in could lead to a quick score at the other end.

The post player, 05, always takes the ball out of bounds on a made field goal because he is the closest to the ball when the other team scores. When a basket is made, 05 retrieves the ball, sprints several strides along the baseline till he sights his primary receiver, and throws the ball to 01 on the left outlet area (Diagram 11-18). 01 has the option to pass to 03 down the sideline, pass to 02 breaking to the middle lane, or dribble down the middle himself. 04 fills the right outside lane, and if a break does not develop, he sprints to the block ballside. 05 fills the weakside block and the offense is ready to go, either from the wing or point (Diagram 11-19).

LEAD-UP DRILLS TO DEVELOP THE FAST BREAK

The following drills are the fundamental drills used to develop the fast break into a team offense. The drills resemble game conditions as closely as possible. Fast break skills include outlet passing, filling lanes, 2-on-1, and 3-on-2 situations.

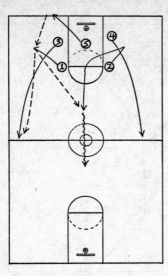

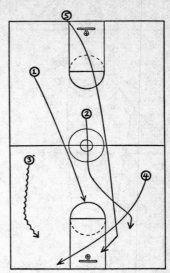

Diagram 11-18   **Diagram 11-19**

Conditioning Fast Break Drills

The four drills allow the team to practice fast break fundamentals and conditioning at the same time. The entire court is used as players are moving up and down both sides continuously. Perform the drills for eight minutes, four minutes each direction. Allow one minute for each drill.

To get the most from these drills, place emphasis on the following:

1. The outlet receiver should always come back to meet the ball.
2. The rebounder should always make the outlet pass a baseball pass or a two-handed overhead pass.
3. Players should fill the proper lanes.
4. Ball handler should always be under control.
5. On made shots, the ball must be taken out of bounds. On missed shots, the ball is rebounded and an outlet pass is made.
6. Rotation is as follows: 01 to 02, 02 to 03, 03 to 04, and 04 to 01.
7. Work toward a goal of 20 made lay-up or 10 made jump shots in each drill.

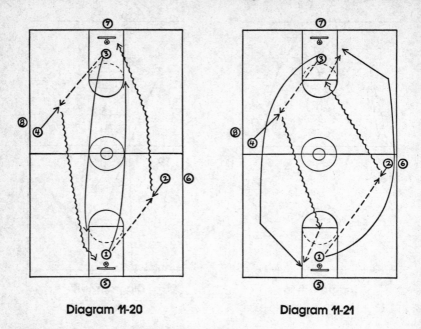

Diagram 11-20   **Diagram 11-21**

Sideline Dribble—Lay-Up and Jump Shot

In Diagram 11-20, players 01 and 03 toss the ball against the backboard, rebound and outlet the ball to 02 and 04 who are breaking back to the outlet areas. After 02 and 04 receive the ball, they dribble hard to the basket and attempt to score a lay-up. 01 and 03, after making the outlet pass, harass the lay-up attempt. If the shot attempt goes in, the next players in each line, 05 and 07, take the ball out of the basket, step out of bounds, outlet the ball to the next receivers, 06 and 08. If the shot misses, the ball is rebounded and outletted.

The drill illustrated in Diagram 11-20, is run again, but this time the players pull up at the wing area (12 feet from basket) and shoot a jump shot.

2-on-1 Break—Lay-Up and Jump Shot

In Diagram 11-21, players 01 and 03 outlet the ball to 02 and 04. 02 and 04, upon receiving the ball, dribble hard down the middle lane. They continue down the middle lane until they reach the foul line where they stop and pass to 01 or 03 for a lay-up. If the shot attempt goes in, the next players in each line, 05 and 07, take the ball out of the basket, step out of bounds, make the outlet pass to the next

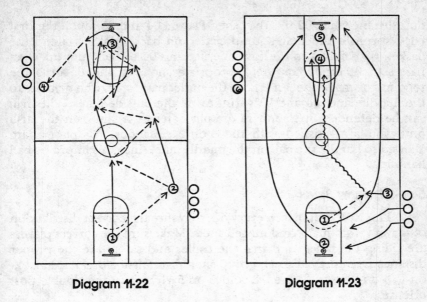

Diagram 11-22   Diagram 11-23

receivers, 06 and 08. If the shot is missed, the ball is rebounded and the outlet pass is made.

The same drill is repeated except, instead of attempting a lay-up, the player on the outside lane stops for a 12-foot jump shot.

2-on-1 Continuous Break

Two lines are formed on each sideline below the hash marks with the first player in each line standing in the middle of the lane, as shown in Diagram 11-22. The drill starts with 01 passing to 02, who has moved to the outlet area. 02 passes back to 01 and continues to move toward the opposite basket as fast as possible. Upon the first pass, 03 sprints out to the center jump circle and backpedals to defend the basket. 01 and 02 attempt a lay-up. They are allowed to dribble when they feel they can score. 03 grabs the rebound or made shot and outlets to 04 and moves up-court. 05 steps out, sprints to center jump circle and defends basket. The drill continues until you are satisfied with the 2-on-1 situation. Demand the lay-up.

3-on-2 Continuous Break

The players line up, as shown in Diagram 11-23. The drill starts with 01 passing to 03, who dribbles up the middle lane. 01 fills one outside lane while 02 fills the other. Players 04 and 05, upon the first pass, sprint to the center jump circle and backpedal to defend the basket. 03 dribbles to the foul line, forcing 04 to pick him up, then passes to 01 or 02 for the appropriate shot. 04 and 05 grab the rebound or made shot and make the outlet pass to 06, who dribbles to the middle lane. 04 and 05 sprint to fill the outside lanes. The drill can be defended by a tandem or split defense. Again, run the drill until you are satisfied with the 3-on-2 situations. All players are allowed to handle the ball on the middle lane, since this improves ball handling.

5-on-0 Dummy Break

This drill is practiced every day to insure the correct distribution of players from made and missed shots. Make sure the correct players are filling the lanes, and that the trailer and safety are the proper distance from the ball.Each group should simulate a break against 2-on-1, 3-on-2, 4-on-3, 5-on-4, and 5-on-5 right into the double post offense.

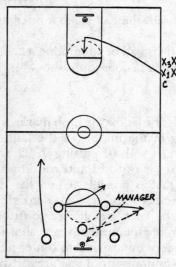

Diagram 11-24

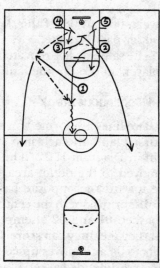

Diagram 11-25

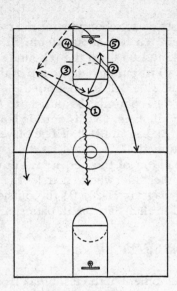

Diagram 11-26

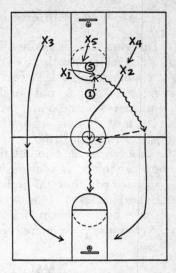

Diagram 11-27

Read-the-Numbers

After the players understand the break, you must provide a means of testing their skills against controlled gamelike situations. Diagram 11-24 shows how to set up the read-the-numbers drill. Take four players to one end of the court and number each one X1, X2, X3, and X4. On the other end, five players set up a 2-3 zone. On your signal, the manager shoots, the group rebounds the ball, outlets it, and proceeds down the court as on a 5-on-0 break. But on the shot, you call out "1," "2," "3," or "4" indicating how many defenders are going to defense the break. The offense never knows what you will call out, so they have to respond to a 2-on-1, 3-on-2, 4-on-3, or 5-on-4 break depending on how many players you send out. This is a tremendous drill for teaching players how to respond to fast break situations.

FAST BREAK FROM A MADE OR MISSED FOUL SHOT

Diagram 11-25 illustrates how to set up to rebound a missed foul shot. Remember that three out of every ten foul shots attempted in high school are missed. Players 03, 04, and 05 form the rebounding triangle and 02 blocks out the shooter. 01 is stationed at the top of the key and moves to the outlet area on the side ball is rebounded.

On missed shots, assuming that 04 rebounds, 04 outlets to 01 who passes to 02 or dribbles to the middle lane. 03 fills outside lane. 05 becomes the trailer, and 04 the safety (Diagram 11-25). The players are now organized as previously mentioned.

On a made shot, 05 grabs the ball out of the net, steps out of bounds and passes to 01 (or 02 on the other side) who in turn looks for 03 on sideline or breaking in middle (Diagram 11-26). 04 fills outside lane. Again, the players are organized in their fast break patterns.

FAST BREAK FROM STEALS

Diagram 11-27 illustrates the development of the fast break from a steal, a loose ball recovery, or when the defense intercepts a pass. Defensive player, X1, intercepts a pass from 01 to 05. X1 immediately dribbles to the outside lane and attempts to get ahead of 01. X2 sprints to fill the middle lane, and X3 fills the outside lane. X4 and X5 become the safety and the trailer. The players are organized in the break as previously described, and attempt to score a quick basket.

If a high percentage shot does not develop, the players will move quickly to a 1-2-2 alignment. The only problem with breaking from a steal is that, occasionally, 04 and 05 could be out of normal fast break organization. In that case, 04 or 05 will pass to the closest perimeter player and quickly assume his post position.

Preparing for
Special Situations in the
DOUBLE POST
Offense

12

The special situations in this chapter add to the total organization of the Double Post Offense, thus providing the little extra preparation needed to win the close games. These special plays can be put in the categories of: center jump situations, under the basket out of bounds, sideline out of bounds, offensive foul situations, and attacking combination defenses.

Each year you should select plays based on the abilities of the players. It is much better to keep these situations simple, so execution of them can be mastered, resulting in an organized and coordinated movement.

CENTER JUMP ALIGNMENT

Several seasons ago we were fortunate enough to have a 6'10" player. Knowing that we had the advantage at the beginning of every quarter to gain four possessions, worth a possible eight points, we established the I alignment. Over the first three seasons we used this alignment, we obtained 87 percent of the tips and scored 60 percent of the time (276 out of 316 tips). Even though we have not had a player of this size since then, outstanding leapers have allowed us to have continued success with this alignment.

In developing our center jump situations, we wanted to: (1) provide an area in which to tip the ball, regardless of the opponent's alignments; (2) create a 2-on-1 or 3-on-2 situation as quickly as possible after the tip is made and then score quickly.

The basic alignment for the center jump is an I alignment, as shown in Diagram 12-1. Place the center, 05, in the center jump circle; this also could be your best leaper. Place the best dribbling wing directly in front of 05 and the other wing, 03, lines up directly behind 05. Place the strong forward, 04, in the mdidle of the free throw line facing 05, and place the point guard in the middle of the opposition's free throw line.

Where the ball is tipped depends upon how the opposition lines up against the I alignment. If the opposition matches your alignment (Diagram 12-1), then you want 05 to tip the ball high and away from the defender guarding 02. 02 should screen his opponent off, receive the ball and drive to the basket. 04, upon seeing 02 receive the ball, should move opposite from 02 to the side of the free throw lane and break to the basket. This creates a 2-on-1 situation that is very difficult to stop. 02 or 04 could score an easy lay-up.

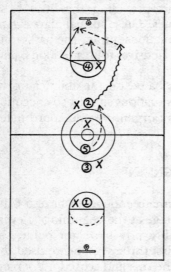
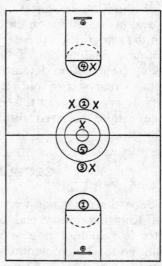

Diagram 12-1   Diagram 12-2

This tip is very simple, yet it puts tremendous pressure on the defense. The opposition is forced to change its player's positions or give up two points. Most teams put a player on each side of 02 to take the direct tip away and place a player beside 03, as shown in Diagram 12-2. When this happens, try to tip the ball to 03 breaking to the side away from his opponent (Diagram 12-3). 03 should receive the ball on

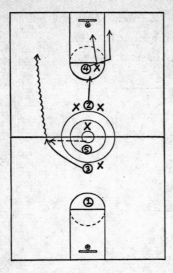

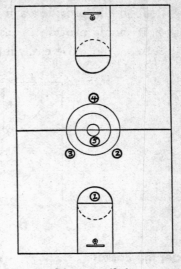

Diagram 12-3   Diagram 12-4

the run and dribble down the sideline looking for an opportunity to drive to the basket. As in the previous situation, 04 breaks to the side opposite the ball and then to the basket. 02 sprints to the free throw line and looks for a return pass. If executed quickly enough, a 3-on-1 or 3-on-2 situation could result.

After teams have seen us play or faced us several times, they take away our opportunity to create a fast break situation. We then become content with gaining possession of the ball. 05 tips the ball back to 01.

If we anticipate losing the tip, the alignment is changed to a Y alignment. (Diagram 12-4). This alignment forces the opponent to tip back, thus allowing us to set up the defense. If a team telegraphs the tip, players are rotated in a direction to attempt a steal.

OUT OF BOUNDS

Many coaches understand the need for a good inbounds play under the basket, but neglect to devise a sideline out-of-bounds play into their system.

A good out-of-bounds play, whether it is under the basket or sideline out of bounds, should meet these three requirements:

1. It should provide a safe means of inbounding the ball.
2. It should provide an easy scoring opportunity.
3. It should move easily into your basic offense.

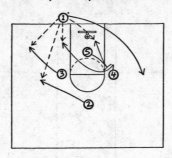

Diagram 12-5

Under the Basket

The alignment for under the basket out of bounds is a diamond (Diagram 12-5). The point, 01, always takes the ball out of bounds; the second guard, 02, assumes a position at the top of key; the best shooting wing, 03, always lines up on the side of 01; 04 lines up opposite 03; and 05 lines up in the middle of the lane. The diamond alignment provides quick scoring plays with screens and cutting movements. The following plays can be run against a man-to-man or zone and on either side of the foul line.

Prior to the official giving 01 the ball, he holds up one finger indicating play one. To start the play, 01 slaps the ball (Diagram 12-5). 05 sets a screen for 04. 04 makes a fake and cuts off the screen to the low-post ballside. After setting the screen, 05 rolls down the lane to the low-post weak side. 03 moves to the corner, while 02 moves laterally from top of key to sidelines, being alert for a five-second violation that might occur because the ball has not been put into play. After passing the ball inbounds, 01 cuts to the wing area.

The following options exist from play one: (1) 01 can pass to 04; (2) 01 can pass to 05; (3) 01 can pass to 03; and (4) as a safety outlet, 01 can pass to 02. If a shot does not develop from the first pass, the ball is passed out to the perimeter if not already there. 05 moves across the lane to high post (Diagram 12-6). This movement places the players in our normal zone offense, Blitz and Rotate, and the offense continues.

Diagram 12-7 illustrates play number two. Play number two is extremely effective against a zone if used sparingly. 01 uses the

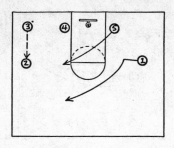

Diagram 12-6

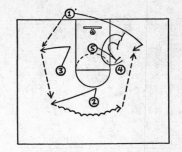

Diagram 12-7

previously described procedure to call the play (two fingers) and start
the play (slaps ball). The play starts the same way as play number one.
05 sets a screen for 04. 04 cuts off the screen and then moves to the
low-post weak side for part of a double screen. 05, after setting the
screen, moves alongside of 04. 01 passes to 03, who in turn passes to
02. 02, upon receiving the ball, dribbles across the key area and passes
to 01 cutting behind the double screen set by 04 and 05. If 01 does not
have a good shot, he passes back out to 02 and the team moves into
their normal zone offense.

Play number three is used vary rarely because we see very little
man-to-man defense on under-the-basket situations (Diagram 12-8).
01 holds up three fingers and slaps the ball to start the play. 04 steps
toward baseline and cuts off 05 to the ball. At the same time, 03 moves
up to screen 02, who cuts off the screen to the sideline area as a safety
valve. After 03's screen, he rolls down the lane using 05 as a screen and
cuts to low-post weak side. If the ball has not been inbounded on these
movements, 05 moves toward the sideline to receive the inbounds
pass. 05, upon receiving the inbounds pass, looks inside for 03 cutting
off 04's screen (Diagram 12-9). This should lead to a lay-up for 03. 02
screens for 01 who breaks toward the ball. If 03 is not open, 05 passes
to 01 at the key area and screens down on 03. This movement puts you
into a 1-2-2 alignment and normal offensive movement continues.

Sideline Out of Bounds

Every team should be prepared to inbounds the ball on the
sideline. The movements of the sideline out-of-bounds plays can be
used anywhere along the sideline. This facilitates the learning of these
plays. Against strong man-to-man pressure, the primary reason for
having such a play is to inbounds the ball safely, and then attempt to
score. The same plays are used against man and zone.

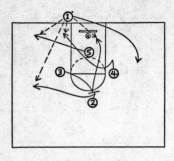

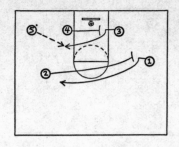

Diagram 12-9

Diagram 12-8

The box alignment is used for the alignment on sidelines out of bounds (Diagram 12-10). A wing is always designated to take the ball out of bounds on the sideline, in this case 02. 03 and 01 are in a straight line with 02, spread approximately 12 to 15 feet apart. 04 and 05 set up in line with the blocks, 12 to 15 feet apart.

As in the under-the-basket play, the ball is slapped to start movement. 02 slaps the ball. 03 turns and sets a screen for 01, who steps down to set his man up and then cuts to the ball. After 03 screens, he rolls back to the ball. At the same time, 05 screens for 04, who cuts across the lane looking for the ball. 02 can pass to 01, 02, and 04 in that order, as shown in Diagram 12-11. After 02 passes to 01, he sprints behind 04 and 05 to the opposite wing area for a pass from 01 who has dribbled to the top of the key. 02 immediately looks to the low post for a pass to 05. 04 moves to low-post weak side, and 03 moves to the left wing area. If 05 cannot be passed to, the regular offense (strong side or weak side) continues.

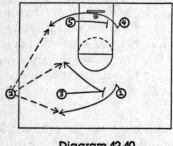

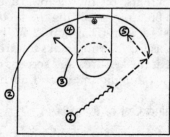

Diagram 12-10

Diagram 12-11

Regardless of where 02 passes, 02 always breaks to the opposite wing area. Diagram 12-12 illustrates these options with a pass from 02 to 04. 02 moves to the left of 04 and cuts over the top for a possible pass from 04. A lay-up usually results. 03 moves to the baseline area after 02 cuts past 04 for a possible pass and jump shot. If no shot develops, the ball is passed out to the perimeter and the offense is aligned in a 1-2-2.

The last sideline out-of-bounds play is used when either there is less than four seconds on the clock at the end of a quarter, or to provide a winning or tying basket at the end of the game.

The players align in the same formation, 02 holds up a closed fist to key the play, and slaps the ball. 03 sets a screen for 01, who breaks towards the ball. 05 and 04 move to set a double screen on the foul line. 03, after setting a screen on 01, cuts down the lane and behind the double screen looking for a pass from 02 (from sideline) or from 01 if play has developed slowly. 03 must shoot when he receives the ball (Diagram 12-13).

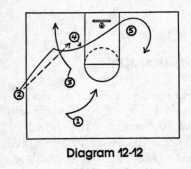

Diagram 12-12

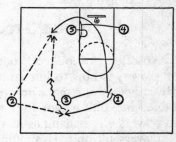

Diagram 12-13

The sideline out-of-bound plays presented are simple and proper execution of them must be stressed at all times. Notice that no special key is used except on the last second shot. The most important point to be emphasized is that the primary purpose is to inbounds the ball.

The previous play is also used to inbounds the ball from the sideline on the defensive end of the court when possession of the ball is of utmost importance. Diagram 12-14 illustrates the proper path of each player. The alignment spreads the defense, and the movements make it tough to prevent an inbounds pass to either 01 or 03. If 03 receives ball on the offensive end of court, 01 must sprint to an area six feet over the center jump circle, expecting a pass from 03. The players move to their areas that start the delay offense.

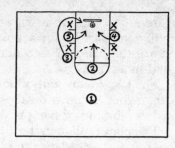

Diagram 12-15

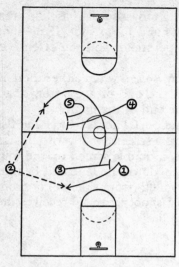

Diagram 12-14

OFFENSIVE FOUL SHOT ALIGNMENT

An often overlooked situation that coaches fail to go over with their players is how to line up on a foul shot on the offensive end. High school players make an average of 60 percent of the shots from the line, and that means four missed shots for every 10 attempted. Drill players on securing as many of those missed shots as possible.

Players 05 and 04 should line up with their feet as close as possible to the lower hash mark. As the ball is released, they should step with the foot closest to the baseline in front of their opponents. Contact should be made while attempting to gain inside position (Diagram 12-15).

Place a third rebounder on the right or left side of the foul lane and just below it. When the ball is shot, the rebounder moves quickly down the foul lane side, anticipating a missed shot. 02 concentrates on making the foul shot first, then rebounding a missed shot. 01 is the defensive safety.

DOUBLE POST DELAY OFFENSE

The alignment for our delay offense is shown in Diagram 12-16. 01 gives the signal (closed fist) and the players move from 1-2-2 set to a

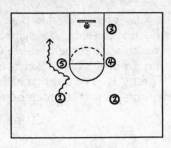

Diagram 12-16

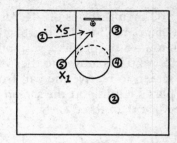

Diagram 12-17

2-2-1 alignment. Visualize 01 dribbling to the left, in line with the side of the foul line; 02 moves from the wing position to the guard position; 03 moves to the low-post area opposite 01; and 04 and 05 move up the lane to high side post.

The delay offense begins when 01 attempts to dribble his defensive player off of a stationary screen set by 05 (Diagram 12-16). It is very important for 05 to make no movement whatsoever while setting the screen for fear of being called for a moving screen. If 01 can rub his man off, he scores on a lay-up. If 05's defensive man, X5, switches to pick up 01, 05 rolls to the basket for a pass from 01 and a lay-up (Diagram 12-17). This dribble movement by 01 usually freezes X5 to play in the lane and prevents a lay-up by 01 or 05.

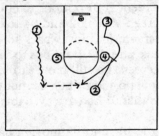

Diagram 12-18

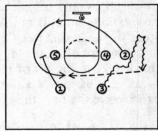

Diagram 12-19

01 should never pick up his dribble until he is absolutely ready to pass. If 01 cannot get a lay-up or screen-and-roll with 05, 01 dribbles back out toward his original position. 02 moves to set a double screen with 04. 03 steps in the lane, then sprints over the double screen to receive a pass from 01, as illustrated in Diagram 12-18. If 03 is overplayed by his defensive man when he reaches the double screen, he immediately cuts backdoor for a pass from 01. If 03 is not open, he moves over the screen to receive the pass from 01.

03 then dribbles off 04, looking for a lay-up or possible pass to 04 (Diagram 12-19). If these situations do not develop, 03 dribbles back toward his original position. 01 moves to set a screen beside 05 for 02, who has moved to the low post away from the ball. 02 cuts off the screen to receive the ball from 03. Timing is very important for the player cutting off the screen to receive the pass. It is much better to be late than to be early.

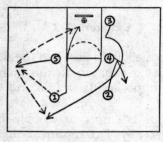

Diagram 12-20

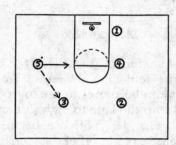

Diagram 12-21

As 01 dribbles, as shown in Diagram 12-19, he is not able to pass to 03, who is breaking off the double screen. 01 fakes a pass toward 03. 05 steps quickly to the wing position to receive a pass from 01. 01 has two options (Diagram 12-20): (1) give-and-go to the basket, or (2) screen for 03 coming off of the double screen. If 01 options to cut to the basket, 03 breaks off of the double screen set by 02 and 04 to the area that 01 vacated. After 02 sets the screen, he moves back to his original position. 01 moves to low-post weak side. If 01 options to set a screen for 03 coming off of the double screen, he still moves to low-post weak side. 02 moves back to his original position. If 03 cannot get open to receive the ball, the same options that 01 had are available to 03.

Diagram 12-21 illustrates 05 passing to 03, and 05 moving back to his post position. The players are back in their 2-2-1 formation, and the offense continues as previously described until a lay-up is attempted or a foul occurs.

If the defense sets up a half-court trap of some sort, set up in a four corner alignment and pass the ball out of the double teams.

Several guidelines must be incorporated for the delay offense to be a success.

1. The players must attempt only lay-ups.

2. Receivers must move quickly to meet all passes.

3. When a player receives a ball, he squares off and faces the defensive player.

4. *Do not* throw crosscourt passes.

ATTACKING COMBINATION DEFENSES

Combination defenses are being employed more and more to neutralize high scoring players and to offset the tempo of successful offenses against normal defenses. This offensive philosophy is based on overall team balance and the correct execution of fundamentals. Since these defenses are exceptions, the best way to attack them is to use the offensive patterns with which the players are already familiar. This can prevent one of the biggest mistakes a coach can make— having a different offense for each defense that might be encountered.

To prepare the team for combination defenses, at least mentally, each defense must be illustrated and defined so that the players know what the defense is attempting to do.

The Double Post Offense can attack the box and one and the triangle and two because it forces the defense to cover the post area, thus allowing more room for the perimeter players.

Attacking the Box and One

This defense is used to stop one outstanding offensive player by playing him man-to-man, but playing the remaining four players in a box zone. The object of the defense is to cut down on the number of possessions the star player gets and to force the remaining players to shoot outside shots. This defense is weak against penetration in the gaps and against good shooters.

We have two methods of confronting the box and one. The first method is used when the player being guarded is one of the post men, 04 and 05. The zone offense, Blitz and Rotate, is used. The players will align themselves in a 1-3-1 set with the post player being guarded at high post. This set attacks the defense in a similar fashion to the way a 2-1-2 zone is attacked. The point should make an effort to penetrate the gap. The zone offense will be run normally, with players looking for shots from the wing area and high-post area as 05 moves to low

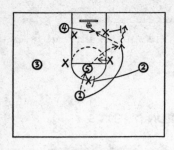

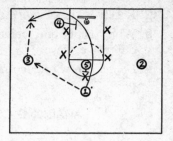

Diagram 12-22   Diagram 12-23

post when the ball is reversed to the other side of the court. Also, the ball is taken to the corner to allow 05 to post up. If the defense sags to prevent all penetration, the offense must be very patient and take only high percentage shots.

Since most of the time the box and one is used against a scoring perimeter player, point or wing, place the top scorer in different positions. The 1-3-1 has been the most successful alignment against this defense. First, attack the defense with the normal zone offense, Blitz and Rotate. The success of the defense will determine what other options are used.

One of the first adjustments is to move the top scorer to the point position, forcing the defense to have a 1-2-2 alignment. Sometimes this alone creates enough scoring opportunities. Diagram 12-22 illustrates 01 passing to 05, forcing the defensive guards, X1 and X2, to collapse. 02 moves to set a screen on 01's defensive man, X1. 01 takes a step to the left and breaks over the screen. 05 passes to 01, who has the option of shooting or passing to 04 breaking to ballside low post, depending on what X4 does. In Diagram 12-23, 01 passes to wing, 03, and cuts down the middle of the lane to the corner on strong side, using 04 or 05 as a screen to free himself. If no shot develops, the zone offense continues.

The second adjustment is to place the top scorer at the wing position. Diagram 12-24 shows 02, the top scorer, cutting off a screen set by 01 after 01 passes to 05 or 03. This movement by 02 sets up his defensive man, X2, to utilize the previous two screens described in Diagrams 12-22 and 12-24. Diagram 12-25 shows 02 after receiving the ball, dribbling off a screen set by 04 for a pick-and-roll.

These options, added with the normal movement of the Blitz and Rotate zone offense, should successfully help you to handle the box and one defense.

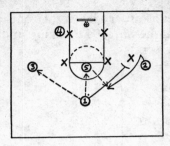

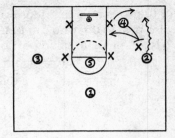

Diagram 12-24   **Diagram 12-25**

Attacking a Triangle and Two

The purpose of this defense is to pressure two perimeter players by playing them man-to-man (switching and trapping) and develop a strong defense around the basket for rebounding purposes. It is important for the two offensive players being guarded to keep their defensive players occupied. The defense is weak in the gap and vulnerable to good outside shooting.

To attack the triangle and two, incorporate several slight adjustments to the Blitz and Rotate zone offense. Place the two players being guarded man-to-man on the perimeter, forcing the bottom portion of the defense to play zone and top man-to-man. The players will set up in a 1-3-1 alignment.

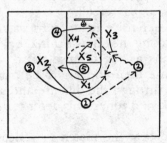

Diagram 12-26

First attack the defense with the normal offense except for exchange between the two players being guarded man-to-man, 01 and 03. Diagram 12-26 illustrates 01 passing to 02 and screening 03, who sets up his defensive man and breaks to the point area. 02 dribbles to the basket until the defensive player, X3, takes him. 02 passes to 04 breaking across the lane to low-post ballside or passes to 03 breaking off of 01's screen. The offense continues as usual against the zone. 01 can also pass to 05, who can pass to 02 at the wing, 04 breaking under the basket, or 03 breaking off of 01's screen.

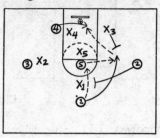

Diagram 12-27

In Diagram 12-27, 01 passes to 05. 02 screens 01's defensive man and 05 passes to 01 breaking off the screen. 01 can shoot a jump shot, or pass to 04. The zone offense will continue normally.

Attacking the Match-Up Zone

The match-up zone defense, if properly executed, is one of the most difficult defenses to attack successfully. The match-up defense combines the strength of zone and man-to-man defenses—denying passes from players one pass away from the ball and helping with zone principles away from the basketball.

Most match-up defensive teams start each possession in their zone defense, thus making the offense think they are attacking a zone. But the trouble begins as the offense passes the ball around the perimeter. The defense then appears to be man-to-man. Then the offense sends cutters through the defense and attempts to screen it. Now the defense is playing zone. This defense can be very confusing to the players.

The best way to beat the match is to beat it back downcourt before the defense sets up by fast breaking and taking high percentage shots.

To attack the match-up, three principles must be instilled in the players. They are: movement, cutting to and away from the ball, and attacking the defense in different areas and with different methods.

If the offensive players just stand around, the defense will have an easy time staying matched up. It is imperative to move, thus forcing defensive adjustments. Having players cut to and away from the ball

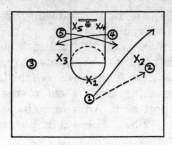

Diagram 12-28

(strongside or weakside cuts) will force the defense to move from space to space. The zone offense and man offense are very similar and allow the players to attack the defense in a variety of ways.

When the players are confronted with a match-up zone, the players align themselves in a 1-2-2 formation. The point, 01, passes to wing, 02, then cuts to the strongside corner. At the same time posts 04 and 05 interchange (Diagram 12-28), and 05 moves up the lane to the side high post. Occasionally, 01 might be open if confusion occurs on defensive assignments. Wing, 02, then has several options: (1) look to high post, but a good match will defend this area successfully; (2) skip pass to 03 if he is a consistent outside threat; (3) pass to 01 in the corner. If 02 passes to 01, his defender, X2, must take away his give-and-go, or give up a lay-up with a return pass from 01 (Diagram 12-29). Diagram 12-30 illustrates post, X5, sagging to help X2 and X3, picking up the cutter at lane area. If X5 sags too far down the lane, 05 can cut to the low-post block for a pass from 01, or 04 can flash to the high post for a pass from 01.

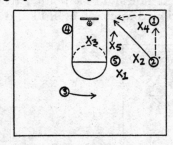

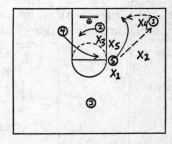

Diagram 12-29   **Diagram 12-30**

Another option for 01 is, upon receiving the ball from 02, he immediately dribbles to the wing area and passes to 03 at the point. At the same time, post, 04, screens X3, and wing, 02, receives a pass from 03 for a jump shot (Diagram 12-31).

Continuing from Diagram 12-30, 01 dribbles to wing, passes to 03, who in turn passes to 02 at the opposite wing. 05 has moved across the lane to ballside low post. 04 moves down the lane to low-post weak side. The offense continues with a cut to the corner by 03 and interchange of both post men. After interchanging, the onside post moves high (Diagram 12-32). These multiple cuts should create an opening in the defense.

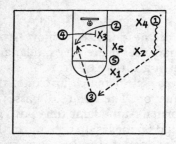

Diagram 12-31

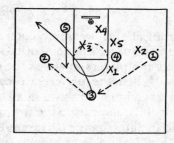

Diagram 12-32

An alternate method used to attack the match would start from the double stack alignment (Diagram 1-5), and then become the normal Blitz and Rotate zone offense, which works to reverse the ball as quickly as possible. This alignment forces the defense into man-to-man coverage, since they must cover the basket area first.

Diagram 12-33 illustrates point, 01, passing to wing, 02, from behind the stack. Post, 04, posts up low while post, 05, flashes to the high post. Wing, 03, remains on the weak side and 01 at point. Any of the previously described options mentioned in chapters 9, 10 and 11 are available to the offense.

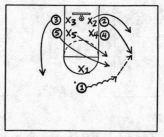

Diagram 12-33

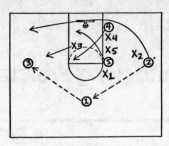

Diagram 12-34

Diagram 12-34 shows a quick reversal by wing, 02, passing to point, 01, who in turn passes to wing, 03. Post 04 and 05 execute their high-low crossing technique, while 02 sprints to the ballside corner to form the box. The cut by 02 will force X4 to cover the corner or have a free shot. If 05 does not cover the low-post area quickly enough, 03 passes to 05 for a power move or he passes to 04 at high post. The offense continues forming the box.

Attacking Pressure Defenses with the

13

DOUBLE POST

Offense

Each year more and more teams are incorporating full-court pressure. It becomes necessary to have an effective method of breaking the press, both half and full. Since there are a large variety of presses being used, it is important to develop a successful press offense that will attack different situations.

In preparing for defensive pressure, you should be ready to be pressed every game and should prepare the team psychologically not to be upset by pressing defenses. One of the first teaching steps for your players should be establishing confidence to handle different presses by providing an organized method to move the ball up-court.

BASIC PRINCIPLES FOR ATTACKING PRESSURE

1. The primary concern is inbounding the ball. Always designate one player to take the ball out of bounds, so as to avoid confusion.
2. Get the ball inbounds before the defense can set up.
3. Be patient and attack under control.
4. All passes should be crisp and no longer than 10 to 12 feet.
5. Dribble more against man than zone. Use dribbling only to attack or advance the ball.
6. Come to meet all passes.

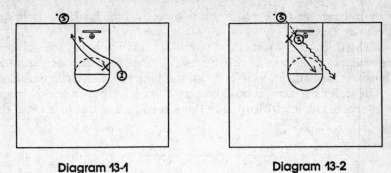

Diagram 13-1   **Diagram 13-2**

INBOUNDING THE BALL

Teach this press offense initially against a man-to-man defense. You must first teach the players several methods of getting open to receive the inbounds pass.

The first method of inbounding the ball is by using a two-guard front (Diagram 13-1). The receiver lines up on the side of the foul line and away from the inbounds passer. He then breaks toward the ball. If he cannot get open, he takes the defensive man to the baseline. Notice that the defensive man is on his back. The inbounds player, 05, bounce passes the ball to receiver (Diagram 13-2). 01 dribbles the ball up the floor against pressure.

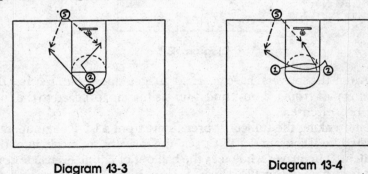

Diagram 13-3   **Diagram 13-4**

The second method of inbounding the ball is using three players, two of which are set in tandem as shown in Diagram 13-3. The back man in the tandem, 01, breaks first and 02 breaks opposite. 05 passes ball inbounds and dribbles up the middle of the court. 05 fills the open lane, sprints up-court, and looks to come back and help out if dribbler needs it.

The third and last method of inbounding the ball is the split set, illustrated in Diagram 13-4. 01 moves across the lane, screens 02's defensive man, and then rolls down the lane to receive the ball from 05. The defensive man should be on 01's back if he set a good screen. An alternate cut for 01 is to fake the screen and V out to receive the ball.

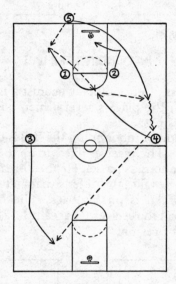

Diagram 13-5

After the players have learned to get open and receive the inbounds pass from a 2-on-2 and 3-on-3 situation, proceed to the five-man press offense.

In breaking the full-court press, start from a 1-2-2 alignment, as illustrated in Diagram 13-5. Coach the players to move into this alignment. The player who takes the ball out of bounds is usually one of the post men, 04 or 05, whichever one is the best passer and ball handler. (I prefer 05 to take the ball out of bounds because he is closest to the basket, and also because we start our fast break with 05 inbounding the ball. He is taught to take the ball out of bounds on one side of the basket.)

Players 01 and 02 set up on each side of the foul line so they will have 15 feet to make a move to get open. 03 and 04 set up on each side of half court. Note that this is the same way to start the fast break from a made basket, which makes the alignment easier to comprehend.

OFFENSIVE METHODS IN ATTACKING FULL-COURT PRESSURE

To simplify the attack against man and zone full-court press, three basic patterns are used to advance the ball up-court. The only difference is in what the player taking the ball out of bounds does. The inbounds passer is provided with three possible cuts which key the pattern. These cuts are pass and away, pass and hold, and strongside cut.

You want a good ball handler advancing the basketball up the court, but you don't want him isolated. A player should always be behind the line of the ball so the dribbler can pass his way out of trouble.

The three patterns all start from the same alignment (Diagram 13-5), and the principles of attack are the same. The objective is to create a fast break opportunity, but if this is not available, to advance the ball up the court.

Against full-court man-to-man, the primary concerns are inbounding the ball to the best ball handler, clearing the other players, and advancing the ball up-court. If the defense utilizes run and jump tactics, the clearing players move to the secondary options used in attacking a zone press.

Pass and Away

This pattern begins with 05 inbounding to 01 who is cutting to get open (Diagram 13-5). Players 01 and 02 can use any method previously described and illustrated to get open to receive the ball, but must balance up after it is inbounded. The ball should be on one side of the lane or the other and not under the basket.

After the ball has been inbounded, the inbounds passer, 05, will step inbounds and move to a position on the weak side of the floor near half-court. At the same time, the weakside guard, 02, breaks to the middle of the lane, and 04 (on the weak side) will flash into the area around the top of the key. 03 holds his position (Diagram 13-5). When 01 receives the ball, he immediately pivots and faces the defense before doing anything else. The reason for this is that you do not want

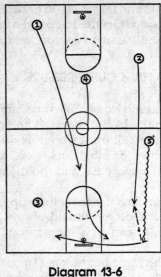 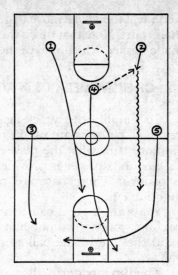

Diagram 13-6   **Diagram 13-7**

a charging foul, with a resulting turnover. Also, 01 should be thinking pass rather than dribble.

The first pass 01 should look to make is to 04 breaking to the key area, and if he is open, the basketball should be passed to him. 04, upon receiving the ball, should be looking for two particular passes, one of which is 05 breaking up the sideline at half-court (Diagram 13-5). With the basketball on the sideline, 05 can dribble down the sideline or pass to 03 breaking to the basket. If 05 should decide to dribble down the sideline to the corner, 02 moves to the wing area on 05's side, 04 sprints to low-post ballside, 01 fills middle lane, and 03 assumes weakside wing (Diagram 13-6). After 05 passes the ball out, he moves to the weakside post to begin the offense. Diagram 13-7 illustrates that 04's other possible pass would be made to 02. 02 dribbles the ball up the sideline. 05 moves down the right, anticipating a pass. If he does not receive a pass, he moves to low-post weak side. 04, after passing to 02, fills middle lane until he reaches foul line, and then proceeds to low-post ballside. 03 fills outside left lane, and 01 is the safety valve ending up at top of key. If a fast break situation is not present, the players are in their normal positions, and the offense will be initiated.

If the defense denies the pass to 04, then the ball should be passed to 02, moving behind the line of the ball. 04 maintains his

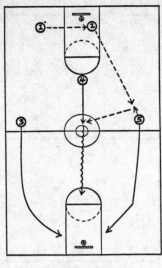

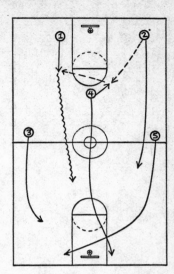

Diagram 13-8   Diagram 13-9

position in the middle. 03 will break down the left lane. 02 can dribble down the sideline and pass to 05, who can pass to 04 breaking down the middle lane to form a three-lane break (Diagram 13-8). 02 can also pass to 04 in the middle who in turn passes to 01 (Diagram 13-9). Now the same offensive series can be repeated on the other side of court.

This is the basic pattern to use against full-court pressure. The proper sequence is to inbounds the ball safely, make a quick pass to the middle, and attack with a fast break.

Occasionally, quick passes into the heart of the defense are not always available because the defense has sagged to prevent them. 01 or 02, whoever has the basketball, dribbles up the court until the defense traps or prevents penetration; then he passes to the trailing guard who is staying behind the line of the ball. 03, 04, and 05 move slowly down the floor, keeping the same distance between the offensive set (Diagram 13-10). This procedure continues until the ball reaches half-court. If a quick pass is made to the middle and passed back to a trailing guard, the fast break attack that was described previously is used.

If 05 cannot make the inbounds pass to 01 or 02, 04 breaks down the middle to receive the ball. 04 passes back to 01 or 02 and the press offense continues (Diagram 13-11).

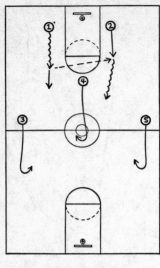

Diagram 13-10

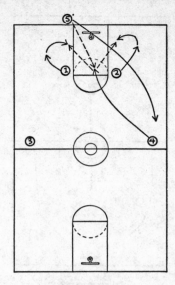

Diagram 13-11

Pass and Hold

The second pattern, pass and hold, aligns the players in a 1-3-1 set after 05 inbounds the ball to 01 (Diagram 13-12). The start of this pattern is the same as pass and away, except after 05 inbounds the ball to 01, he steps inbounds and stops. This keys the pattern. 02, upon reading 05's move, moves to an area between foul line extended and half court. 04 flashes to the middle lane, and 03 moves to the other end of the court. Upon receiving the ball, 01 turns and faces the defense, looking for 04 in the middle lane. 04 then passes to 03 breaking up the sideline (Diagram 13-12). 02 dribbles down the sideline with 04 sprinting down the middle lane to low-post ballside, while 01 fills the middle lane as a trailer and stops at top of key. 03 stays on the weak side away from the ball. 05 is the trailer and moves to low-post weak side if a fast break shot does not develop.

If 01 cannot pass to 04 in the middle lane, he passes to 05 behind the line of the ball (Diagram 13-13) and moves to a position opposite of 02. The players will maintain the 1-3-1 alignment while advancing the ball downcourt with quick passes and dribbling. Diagram 13-13 illustrates 05 passing to 02 on the sideline, who in turn passes to 04 in the middle. 04 passes to 01 breaking up the sideline, who in turn

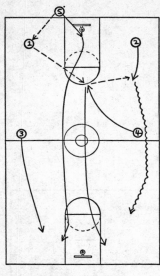

Diagram 13-12

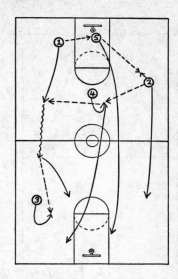

Diagram 13-13

passes to 03, and then moves to the middle lane. 04 then breaks to low-post ballside, 02 moves to the weakside wing area, and 05 trails and then moves to low-post weak side. The pass and hold provides a safe method of advancing the ball against full-court pressure.

Strongside Cut

The strongside cut is used against zone pressure with 05 making a strongside cut behind 01 after inbounding the ball to him. 02 moves to an area in the lane behind the line of the ball. 04 flashes to the middle lane, close to the center jump circle area. 03 breaks down the sideline. 01 waits for a possible double team and looks in the middle. 04 passes to 02 breaking down the sideline (Diagram 13-14). 02 dribbles down the sideline and 04 breaks down the middle lane to low-post ballside. 01 trails and fills middle lane, while 05 sprints to low-post weak side (Diagram 13-15). This is a quick hitting attack that creates a lot of fast break opportunities.

If 01 cannot pass to 05 on the strong side, he passes to 02 behind the line of the ball (Diagram 13-16). 02 dribbles downcourt looking to pass to 04 in the middle. 04 passes to 01 breaking up the sideline. Upon seeing the ball reversed, 03 moves to the other side of court

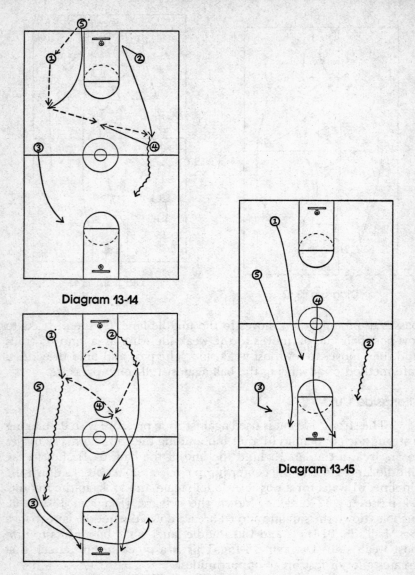

Diagram 13-14

Diagram 13-15

Diagram 13-16

(wing area). 01 dribbles the ball down the sideline, 05 sprints down the sideline and then moves to low-post ballside, and 04 breaks down middle lane and moves to low-post weak side. 02 trails and fills middle lane.

OFFENSE METHODS IN ATTACKING HALF-COURT PRESSURE

In the last several years the use of half-court trapping defenses has increased, due mainly to the fact that these defenses are easier to play because there is less court area to defend. Do not consider a straight half-court man-to-man press as a half-court press; your players should be able to attack the defense with a normal offense. It is only the trapping defenses with which you should be concerned here.

To attack half-court pressure, two different alignments are used. Which one is used depends on the particular type of defense being used. Although the alignments are different, the principles of the attack are similar: look for the quick pass and try to create a fast break situation.

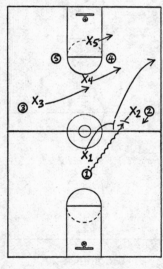

Diagram 13-17

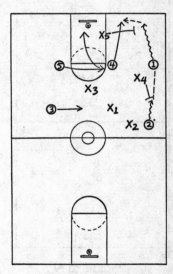

Diagram 13-18

Blitz and Rotate Half-Court Attack

To attack a 1-2-1-1 half-court trap, a 1-4 alignment is used. Utilizing the two basic zone attacks facilitates learning how to attack this defense. The strongside cut and hit-the-pivot plays are used.

Diagram 13-17 illustrates 01 dribbling into the trap set by X1 and X2, passing to 02, and making a strongside cut. An important coaching point for 02 is not to move away from 01, making 01 pass over or around X2. Upon receiving the ball, 02 dribbles, forcing X4 to stop him so that he cannot defend 01 (Diagram 13-18). 02 picks up his dribble and has two possible options: (1) 01 on the sideline, or (2) 05 flashing into the middle. As 02 is dribbling, 04 breaks to low-post ballside, and 03 moves to the high-post area as a safety valve.

In 02's first option, he passes to 01, who in turn dribbles toward the baseline, attempting to draw X5 to him. 01 passes to 04 for a shot. If 01 cannot pass to 04 stationed at low-post ballside, 01 passes to 02 at the wing area, and moves to the opposite wing area as in our regular zone offense (Diagram 13-19).

In the second option, 02 passes to 05, 05 can shoot, drive, or pass to 04 at low post, or to 01 breaking toward baseline, or to 03 on the weak side (Diagram 13-20). If no shot develops, the regular zone offense continues until a shot develops.

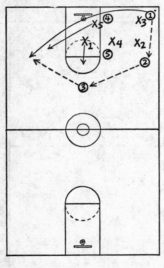
Diagram 13-19

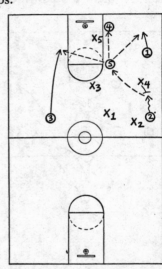
Diagram 13-20

Diagram 13-21 illustrates the second option of 01—hit-the-pivot—when he has dribbled into the trap set by X1 and X2. This penetrating pass usually results in creating a fast break situation (3-on-2). 01 passes to 04, stepping up in the middle of the defense. 04 immediately turns, making sure not to put the ball on the floor, which could cause a charge and thus miss an open player around the basket. 04 looks to pass to 05 breaking towards the basket or 02 breaking backdoor.

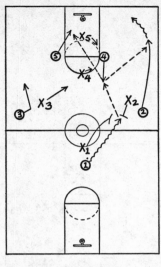

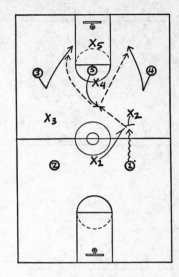

Diagram 13-21   **Diagram 13-22**

2-3 Half-Court Attack

The second attack used against half-court defenses is a 2-3 attack (Diagram 13-22). As 01 dribbles toward the trap to be set by X1 and X2, he is reading the defense for three possible passes. 02 stays behind the line of the ball, while 03, 04 and 05 move higher on the floor. The three areas of attack are: (1) pass to the middle of defense, (2) pass to the forward in the high wing area, and (3) pass to 02 on the weak side. These passes will depend on the movements of defensive players X3 and X4.

In the first option, 01 passes to 05 in the middle of the defense creating an immediate fast break situation (3-on-2). 05 immediately turns, looking to pass to 04 or 03, who is breaking toward the basket. 05 should not dribble the ball. If the defense shifts to prevent this pass from 01 to 05, 04 goes to basket while 05 moves to the area 04 vacated, and 03 flashes into the middle of defense (Diagram 13-23). 01 passes to 02, who immediately turns and looks to pass to 04 breaking to the basket or 02 going backdoor. If 01 passes to 05, 05 can pass to 03 in middle, 04 at low post, or 02 on the weak side (Diagram 13-24).

In the second option, 01 passes to 04 in the high wing area (Diagram 13-25). 04 has the option of passing to 05 breaking to low

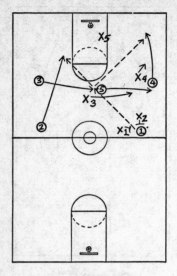

Diagram 13-23

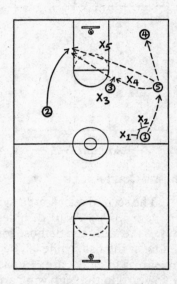

Diagram 13-24

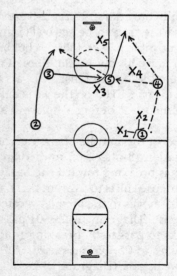

Diagram 13-25

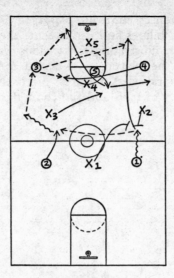

Diagram 13-26

post, 03 flashing high or 02 going backdoor on weak side. Usually a shot develops; if not, the regular zone offense takes over.

The third option goes into effect when the first two options are not available to 01 because the defense is covering all the lanes on the ballside of court. 01 reverses the ball to 02, who passes to 03. 03 has the option of passing to 05 breaking to low post, 04 flashing high, or 01 going backdoor (Diagram 13-26).

Both half-court zone attacks are simple, and yet provide an effective means of providing ball possession and scoring opportunities.

Installing the Press Attack

Use the team approach in installing both the half- and full-court press attack, since these options require coordination involving all five players. Do not use a series of drills, but teach the offense starting with the proper alignment. The offensive patterns and available options are explained thoroughly throughout this book. Then, go over the offense without defenses until all players are familiar with their position and responsibilities and can execute them full speed. Then use a token defense, illustrating the various ways the defense will attack them. Once the players understand the movement of the defense and understand what the press offense is attempting to do, try it against a variety of half- and full-court defenses.

MASTER PRACTICE PLAN

I. Basic skills

A. Offense
  1. Ball handling
     a. Pound the ball
     b. Finger tip drill
     c. Pass ball around ankles, waist and head
     d. Single leg circle
     e. Combination—around legs and body
     f. Figure-eight between legs
     g. Figure-eight with drop
     h. Side catch
     i. Front catch
     j. Spin ball
     k. Dribble around one leg
     l. Dribble figure-eight around legs
     m. Front pockets
     n. Side pockets
     o. Back pockets
     p. Crab run
  2. Dribbling
     a. Speed dribble
     b. Change of pace
     c. Crossover
     d. Between the leg
     e. Behind the back

   f. Reverse
   g. Fake reverse
  3. Passing
   a. Two-hand chest pass
   b. Two-hand bounce pass
   c. Two-hand overhead pass
   d. Baseball pass
   e. Flip pass
  4. Shooting
   a. Lay-up
   b. Hook shot
   c. Jump shot
   d. Foul shot
  5. Fakes and drives
   a. Jab and shoot
   b. Jab and go
   c. Jab and crossover
   d. Combine these moves with dribbling moves
  6. Movement without ball
   a. Backdoor cut
   b. V cut
   c. Hook cut
   d. Reverse
  7. Rebounding
   a. Back spin and roll
   b. Fake and go opposite

B. Defense
  1. Stance
  2. Movement
   a. Advance step
   b. Retreat step
   c. Swing step
  3. Guard a player with a basketball
   a. Baseline drive
   b. Side to middle drive
   c. Middle to side drive
  4. Guard a player without a basketball
   a. One pass from ball
   b. Two passes from ball
   c. Fronting post

II. Team concepts

A. Offense
  1. Fast break
     a. Rebounding
     b. Outlet
     c. Distribution
     d. Situations
     e. From a made field goal
     f. From a foul shot situation
  2. Two-man situations
     a. Give-and-go
     b. Backdoor
     c. Pass and screen ball
     d. Weakside play
     e. Single cuts off the post
     f. Go behind
  3. Three-man situations
     a. Pass and screen opposite
     b. Split the post
     c. Post
     d. Clear
     e. High-post rub
  4. Team patterns
     a. Strongside series
     b. Weakside series
     c. Post series
     d. Clear series

B. Defense
  1. Two-on-two situations
     a. Give-and-go
     b. Pick-and-roll
     c. Single cuts off post
     d. Go behind
     e. Flash cuts
  2. Three-on-three situations
     a. Pass and away (fight over screen)
     b. Split the post
     c. Shuffle cut
  3. Four-on-four situations

      a. Positional play
      b. Give-and-go
      c. Flash pivot
      d. Run and jump
      e. Trap
   4. Five-on-five situations
      a. Against a 1-2-2 alignment
      b. Against a 1-3-1 alignment
      c. Against a 2-1-2 alignment
   5. Zones
      a. 2-3 zone
      b. Match-up zone
   6. Team defense (full court)
      a. Full-court man-to-man
      b. Full-court zone press (1-2-1-1)
      c. Half-court zone press (1-2-1-1)

III. Situations

A. Center jump "I" or "Y"
B. Under the basket out of bounds
C. Sideline out of bounds
D. Double post stall
E. Foul shot alignments and situations

Index

Dan Dunn.